Consumption

Consumption

Ian Hudson
Mark Hudson

polity

First published in 2021 by Polity Press

Polity Press
65 Bridge Street
Cambridge CB2 1UR, UK

Polity Press
101 Station Landing
Suite 300
Medford, MA 02155, USA

ISBN-13: 978-1-5095-3537-8
ISBN-13: 978-1-5095-3538-5 (pb)

A catalogue record for this book is available from the British Library.

Library of Congress Cataloging-in-Publication Data
Names: Hudson, Ian, 1967- author. | Hudson, Mark, 1971 June 27- author.
Title: Consumption / Ian Hudson, Mark Hudson.
Description: Cambridge, UK ; Medford, MA : Polity Press, 2021. | Series: What is political economy? | Includes bibliographical references and index. | Summary: "A crystal-clear guide to how consumption greases the wheels of modern capitalism"-- Provided by publisher.
Identifiers: LCCN 2020024396 (print) | LCCN 2020024397 (ebook) | ISBN 9781509535378 (hardback) | ISBN 9781509535385 (paperback) | ISBN 9781509535392 (epub)
Subjects: LCSH: Consumption (Economics) | Capitalism.
Classification: LCC HB801 .H83 2021 (print) | LCC HB801 (ebook) | DDC 339.4/7--dc23
LC record available at https://lccn.loc.gov/2020024396
LC ebook record available at https://lccn.loc.gov/2020024397

Typeset in 10.5 on 12pt Sabon
by Fakenham Prepress Solutions, Fakenham, Norfolk NR21 8NL
Printed and bound in Great Britain by CPI Group (UK) Ltd, Croydon

For further information on Polity, visit our website:
politybooks.com

Contents

Acknowledgements

This book benefited tremendously from the behind-the-scenes work of talented people whose names don't appear anywhere on the front cover. We would like to thank two anonymous reviewers for their careful reading and helpful comments. The team at Polity, particularly George Owers, Julia Davies, Evie Deavall, and Caroline Richmond, were also constructive and patient as we went through the writing process. Finally we would like to extend a huge thank you to our three excellent research assistants: Katherine Burley, Rylan Ramnarace and Jillian Stefanson. The money to hire them came from the Undergraduate Research Award program and the Faculty of Arts' Global Political Economy Research Fund, University of Manitoba.

1
The Meanings of Consumption

Coachella is a music and arts festival that happens every April in the city of Indio, California. Coachella is so cool, so self-explanatory that the answer to the number one question on the website's FAQ "But Why?" is "Because." Its 2019 music headliners featured heavy hitters such as Ariana Grande. It puts the festive in festival with the Pantene Styling Lounge, which encourages people to "be at the top of your content game & get your hair styled with glittery gold accessories," and the "Sound + Sun = Fun" experience, where "Wearing Bose Frames & pairing them with your phone doesn't just give you music for hours & style for miles – it also unlocks exclusive audio content in the official Coachella app." Its 2019 sponsor list runs from Absolut and Amazon to Uber and YouTube. The UK's Sun deemed Coachella "one of the most 'FOMO'-inducing events of the year" (Wakefield, 2019). For those, like ourselves, who need the urban dictionary to understand even outdated terms, FOMO is fear of missing out – the anxiety you experience from missing a crucial event, often brought on by viewing posts on social media.

Part of the story of Coachella revolves around the importance of the festival as a vehicle for marketing. The sponsors not only appear prominently on the webpage but they are integrated into the very event itself, putting their names on parties and activities. This may represent a change from some concerts of the distant past, such as Woodstock, but this marketing path has been well travelled by big events such as Lolapalooza, which debuted way back in 1991.

What is also notable about Coachella and many similar culturally important events is that they are no longer merely events that people enjoy as consumers. They are also inputs into the production of something that had barely been conceived when Lolapalooza first grunged its way on stage. The 2019 Coachella festival was attended by the likes of Kendall Jenner, Olivia Culpo, Hailey Bieber, Gigi Hadid and Emma Chamberlain, some of the biggest influencers in the world. To take one from the list, Emma Chamberlain is an eighteen-year-old who, in 2019, had 8 million YouTube subscribers and another 7.7 million followers on Instagram. By some estimates she was earning around $2 million from the ads on her YouTube channel alone (Lorenz, 2019). Her product, distributed on social networks such as Instagram, YouTube and Twitter, is herself, or at least an infotainment version of her life. Influencers like Chamberlain make money by signing contracts with brands eager to have their products associated with people's real life stories. Of course, the more followers an influencer has, and the better able they are to create sales for their sponsors, the bigger the contract. Chamberlain, for example, has a partnership with Hollister, which involves her posing for Instagram posts in its clothes. Our interest in their daily lives really functions – from their point of view and that of their sponsoring companies – only to make us into more enthusiastic consumers.

Influencers are not only selling their public lives to promote consumption, but their ability to do so is determined by the creation of an aspirational, interesting and enviable lifestyle through the products that they consume. So their status is largely based on the careful curation of their own consumption. For an influencer, whose stock-in-trade is living a life that others want, a media feed without Coachella is an incomplete and below average product, like a car without air conditioning. The idea that people are worth following because of the interesting ways they create an identity through consumption demonstrates the increasingly strong connection between who a person is and what they consume.

Influencers also demonstrate how new technologies and platforms are designed for commercial purposes. Instagram was originally touted as a venue for people to share pictures with friends, but it quickly transformed into a marketing tool – both for the collection and sale of data about our consumer preferences to advertisers and as a more traditional advertising venue – in order to maximize its revenue stream. Do influencers represent a worrying new trend in which people famous for doing nothing other than showing off their lives peddle a shallow, materialistic and yet unattainable version of the "good life" to their impressionable followers? Should the idea that someone's life can become a marketable, commercial product give us cause for concern?

What Are We Talking About? Consumption and Political Economy

As its title suggests, this book is about consumption. What the title does not make clear is what we actually mean by that word. Consumption did not always mean what it does now. Back in the day, it meant the "using up" of things, like physical strength, which meant that it was used to describe the exhaustion of the body caused by tuberculosis (Trentmann, 2016). From this definition, it is clear that consumption had something of a negative connotation, associated with wastefulness and tragic wasting away.

The word "consumption" has benefited from a remarkable transformation to become associated with the pleasures of enjoying goods and services such as those offered by Coachella. Different scholars have put forward very different definitions, from the relatively narrow to the very broad. On the very broad end of the spectrum, in the discipline of economics, consumption generally means the use of goods and services by households (McCabe, 2015: 4–5). Historian Frank Trentmann defines consumption as "a shorthand that refers to a whole bundle of goods that are obtained via different systems of provision and used for different purposes" (Trentmann, 2012: 3). This broad definition allows him to place very different goods and services, acquired and used in a wide variety of ways, under the category of consumption. To use his examples, buying a Ferrari and turning on a shower are both consumption activities. For Trentmann, the key difference between the two is that one is a luxury, purchased to display your status in society, and the other is more of a necessity and done without any showy considerations. We might also add that the Ferrari is produced by a for-profit company, while the water that streams out of the shower is, for most people, provided by a utility, owned, controlled or heavily regulated by the government. Clearly, Trentmann's definition can be applied across almost all societies, political economic systems and historical periods. This definition could be used to describe someone in the United States in 2019, buying (or stealing) a digital download, and someone two thousand years ago, eating a root vegetable pulled out of the ground for the communal pot in a hunter-gatherer society.

Those opting for a narrower definition often attempt to distinguish between consumption done in different manners with different motives. Historians Neil McKendrick, John Brewer and J. H. Plumb define consumption in a *consumer society* as taking place in the context of the market, and in which people have sufficient discretionary income to buy for fashion and novelty rather than necessity and durability (McKendrick et al., 1982: 3). An extension of a consumer society's attraction to fashion and novelty added by some scholars is that "wants and needs [are] infinitely stretchable" (Stearns, 2001: 16), so that people are willing to "take up everything that is endlessly produced" (Clarke et al., 2003: 27). This creates a distinction between the motives of people in a pre-consumer society – those who are satisfied with some (admittedly unspecified) level of comforts from consumption – and those in a consumer society – who behave in a manner which reflects what economists define as non-satiation of wants.

Writers taking the role of consumption in defining people's goals and identities one step further often talk about consum-er*ism*, or a consumer society, as one in which "many people formulate their goals in life partly through acquiring goods that they clearly do not need for subsistence or for traditional display" (Stearns, 2001: ix). The addition in this definition is the "formulation of goals in life," so consumption in the context of consumer*ism* is not only about acquiring but also about identifying yourself through what has been acquired. Sociologist Mark Paterson, for example, has a definition of consumerism that appears to be targeted toward the importance of lifestyle considerations: "a particular moment in which the consumer is participating in a series of processes, having taken account of branding, images, notions of self-worth ... and exercised the temporary satisfaction of a desire or felt need" (Paterson, 2017: 3). For Paterson, any examination of current consumption must include "what kinds of things are motivating our decisions to buy, such as the concept of lifestyle, advertising, and notions of consumer choice" (ibid.: 12). This suggests that people define themselves by their consumption – as consumers – rather than through the other roles in their lives. Instead of identifying with their occupation, for example, people view work only as a means "to acquire coveted, meaning-laden consumer items, while the inherent meanings or value attributed to one's work, career, or job largely [loses] importance ... the primary purpose of work [is] its potential or ability to generate disposable income for consumption" (Dholakia and Fuat Firat, 1998: 5). This creates a difference between Trentmann-style consumption, which can be applied fairly universally, a consumer society and consumerism. We use the word "consumerism" to refer to a cultural orientation in which needs are fulfilled and meaning is produced primarily through the acquisition of commodities.

This book gives an analysis of consumption using a political economy framework. This means that it will examine theories through which we can analyze the context for, and consequences of, most consumption as it is currently practiced within a specific system of political economy. Consumption is part of an economic system. Rather than approaching it from the exclusive point of view of the individual consumer, a political economy of consumption centers the systemic: the needs of a capitalist system for growth, the embeddedness of individual consumption in commodity-specific "systems of provisioning" (Fine, 2002: 79), and the problems that arise from those systems for people and the planet. Political economy also foregrounds that consumerism as a mass phenomenon is historically specific. The implication of this is that a political economy of consumption does not set out to generate a critique of "consumption" as a transhistorical or ahistorical category. We must, in some way, shape or form, consume. Rather, we set out to add to our understanding of how capitalism conditions our patterns of consumption in specific ways.

We will take McKendrick et al.'s definition of consumption, which includes the market, one step further by arguing that capitalism – our currently dominant political economic system – contains two other crucial components: for-profit, private ownership and wage labour. Many other political economies, such as slavery, used markets extensively. The key difference between capitalism and slavery is not markets but the different rules about how labour is organized, which have crucial implications for the manner in which consumption should be analyzed. Slaves engaged in consumption – they ate food, wore clothes and slept in shelter of better or often worse quality. They even had some input into the goods and services purchased for their use (McDonald, 2012: 118). However, consumption by the slave, as an owned input into production, would have been determined largely by the slave owner, with the purpose of yielding the highest return in terms of minimizing the cost while maintaining the value of the slave as a salable asset and input in production. In capitalism, for-profit firms hire workers in the labour market based on whether the costs of the worker are less than the benefits that the worker produces for the firm. This calculation largely determines the income that workers have for consumption. The manner in which consumption decisions are made by a wage earner is vastly different in terms of the income earned and the worker's amount of discretion about where that income goes. It is consumption by the worker, rather than the slave, on which this book will focus. It is the "sphere of exchange," or the market, for both labour and consumer goods that translates work into consumption in a capitalist, market economy (Sassatelli, 2007).

The second element that distinguishes the capitalist political economy is for-profit, private ownership. This is relevant in terms of consumption because it means that the goods and services that people consume are produced in order to make a profit for firms and the individuals that own them. Goods and services produced in this manner are often referred to as commodities. This makes for a different context of provision than occurs in the home or by the government, neither of which are quite as concerned with profits. Most people acquire most of their goods and services through the market, although this is not exclusively so. Many goods and services, although a declining percentage of total consumption, are acquired through production in the household. This is where many child-rearing services are performed, from changing diapers to cooking meals, often according to socially constructed, traditionally defined gender roles. People also consume goods and services produced by the government. This is how most people get their education, their drinking water, fire protection and roads. Compared to market provision, these are produced under a different logic and with very different consequences for who gets to consume and the types of goods and services with which those people will be provided. In this book, we are concerned primarily with commodity consumption, although we will frequently contrast its crucial differences with the home or government. To sum up all of our definitional discussion, this book is on consumption, with a particular focus on capitalist, commodity consumption, or, as sociologist Max Weber put it, the satisfaction of daily wants and needs achieved through the "capitalist mode" (Weber, 1961).

Competing Themes in the History of Consumption

As we shall see in the remainder of the book, two fractures show up time and again in analyzing the political economy of consumption. The first tension is whether the evolution of consumption is one of continuity or transformation. Those, like Trentmann, who advocate for continuity argue that consumption is a dynamic evolution, not a phenomenon that should be associated with more recent times or any particular place. Rather, they argue that consumption and consumer culture extend back into time and across geographical locations, with no sharp break between a consumer society and a pre-consumerist past (Trentmann, 2009). As Trentmann stated, "things are an inextirpable part of what makes us human" (2016: 678).

Continuity advocates point to the importance of consumption beyond the usual Western European and American locations and back into the distant past. In tribal societies people not only ate, clothed and sheltered themselves but also consumed beyond bare necessities, often using consumption as a mark of status (Sassatelli, 2007). The Roman Empire was famous for its system of transportation that facilitated trade (Trentmann, 2009: 191). Marco Polo's voyage in the thirteenth century marked the beginning of long-distance trade in high-value items between Asia and Europe. His accounts of the riches of the Great Han, including exotic horses, elephants and leather shoes, inspired further voyages and an expansion of Asian possessions in Europe by the aristocracy and (perhaps ironically) the religious hierarchy – an inventory in 1295 at the Vatican listed quite a collection of Mongolian silk (McCabe, 2015: 18–19). Moving in the other direction, Western imported goods were integrated into Middle Eastern markets by the sixteenth century (Stearns, 2001). An important part of this scholarship highlights the number of things that were in people's houses as evidence of their propensity to consume (Margairaz, 2012: 193). In China, during the late Ming dynasty (up to the first half of the 1600s), books were an important household item, as were Japanese-made fans, lacquered tables, gold-painted screens and cosmetic boxes (Trentmann, 2016: 47).

Even McKendrick et al.'s definition of consumption for novelty and fashion can be found in more locations and further back in time than is often assumed. In Ming China, people exhibited a taste for changing sleeve lengths, demonstrating the importance of fashion, and one scholar at the time lamented that for "young dandies in the villages … even silk gauze isn't good enough and [they] lust for Suzhou embroideries." Merchants would create gigantic banners, some as much as 10 meters high and lit by lanterns at night, to attract customers (Trentmann, 2016: 47). In Zanzibar, off the East African coast, status items such as jewelry and umbrellas were important markers of social standing. Although consumption has evolved, expanded and intensified, it has a much longer history in much more diverse geographic space than is often acknowledged (ibid.: 677).

Similarly, innovations that facilitate consumption, such as credit, also have a long history. Credit is useful because it allows the purchase of more expensive items without prior saving and facilitates continued consumption during temporary periods of reduced income. The Code of Hammurabi in Mesopotamia in 1752 BC laid out the terms of debt bondage in which men could pledge themselves or other family members into the service of a creditor to pay off their debts (a practice that still continues in some countries, such as India). Over time there has been an incredibly wide range of arrangements between debtor and creditor – from those granted based on personal relationships of trust, such as when bartenders would chalk up their drinkers' debts on a slate above the bar until it was wiped clean by payment, to those backed by collateral, such as a pawnshop, to those backed by law, such as the debtor's prison, where creditors could have delinquent borrowers confined until they paid up (Wiedenhoft-Murphy, 2016).

For those that view consumption through the continuity lens, there is rarely such a thing as a new problem. For every perceived disaster seen by analysts focused on current trends, the continuity researcher can point to a historical precedent. For example, the concern that globalization creates problems for local producers and sacrifices local tastes and culture is hardly new. Long-distance trade has been practiced throughout much of the sweep of recorded history. As early as the tenth and eleventh century, a long-distance trade in commodities was well established, with cotton, textiles, spices, silks and curtains being shipped across the Indian Ocean (Trentmann, 2009: 191). The worry that new, low-cost retailers such as Walmart, or, even worse, online sellers such as Amazon, will destroy their competitors also has a historical precedent. The same debates, with the same alarmist tones, occurred in the 1800s, when early department stores used low prices, one-stop shopping and innovative advertising techniques to pioneer purchasing as a recreational activity (Haupt, 2012: 272). Yet small-scale retail survived. Department stores took only 3 percent of total retail by 1914 in Western Europe (Trentmann, 2016: 205). The concern that consumption represents a social failure, in which people vainly attempt to show off and emulate, has been repeated in many different times in many different contexts (ibid.: 677). Centuries ago, in Italy, critics lamented the vanity of the market for beauty products, including fake hair, which was demanded not only by the predictably preening nobility but also by more humble artisans and innkeepers (ibid.: 30).

In contrast, transformationists see sharper breaks in consumption. This does not mean that there are no historical precedents for trends or that there are no antecedents for revolutions in consumption, but that certain periods can be identified as notably different from the past. In one particularly bold example of this, McKendrick et al. (1982) claim that the "birth" of the consumer society could be pinpointed to the third quarter of the 1700s in England, which was the richest country at the time – alternative birthplaces include the seventeenth-century Dutch Republic, Renaissance Italy and seventeenth-century France (McCabe, 2015: 2–3). These authors justified their sharp period break with some impressive statistics. Sales of non-necessities such as soap, candles and beer increased at more than twice the rate of population growth over the last fifteen years of the eighteenth century (McKendrick et al., 1982: 29).

For McKendrick et al., it was not that people's desires for consumption changed, but incomes and prices certainly did. Starting in the 1600s, the expansion of trade and the establishment of agricultural plantations reduced the price of many little pleasures, such as tobacco, tea, coffee and sugar (Pennell, 2012: 75). Coffee gained popularity as a puritanical alternative to alcohol, which improved performance rather than hindering it (Sassatelli, 2007). The use of tobacco also spread widely, famed for its positive medical properties and ability to calm the nerves (McCabe, 2015: 73). The price of sugar dropped so much during the seventeenth century that the consumption of candies was possible for more than just the nobility, and the dessert course was introduced (ibid.: 57–8). According to McKendrick et al., this represented the "democratization" of consumption, in which spending habits that were once the exclusive purview of the very rich spread to the wider masses of the population, creating a consumer society, as opposed to a society that had some consumers (1982: 14). "All other classes imitated as best they could – which was much better than in the past" (ibid.: 11).

Transformationists argue that consumption should not be analyzed through "presentism," which is looking at the past through the lens of, and in preparation for, the present by ascribing motives and values where they might not belong (McCracken, 1987: 142). For McKendrick et al., the revolution of the late 1700s provided people with the income to pursue the consumption that they had always wanted, but for other transformationists the break between the pre- and post-consumer society is also about culture and values in very different political, economic and social contexts. For example, many value systems before the 1700s, often based on religious doctrines from Christianity, to Islam, to Confucianism, were highly critical of worldly affluence and the excessive consumption that it spawned (although this did not prevent the upper levels of the religious and aristocratic hierarchy from living in ostentatious luxury). The earlier evidence on the continuity of consumption from Ming China, for example, needs to be tempered with the fact that most people did not think of themselves as consumers or even greatly value certain types of consumption that were associated with luxury or excess (Clunas, 2012; McCabe, 2015: 1). Different authors point to different periods in which these attitudes started to change. McCracken (1988), for example, points to Queen Elizabeth's ostentatious consumption as a crucial feature of courtly behaviour in sixteenth-century England as one turning point. Generally, for these transformationists, the consumer society was created by a change in society's cultural attitudes around consumption (Stillerman, 2015).

Consumerism was also often at odds with the strong influence of tradition, often reinforced by legal constraints on consumption (Stearns, 2001: 4–9). Sumptuary laws that restricted what people were allowed to own were placed on a shockingly wide range of goods: in fourteenth-century Venice, tapestries could not measure more than 1.5 meters and gilded fireplace furnishings were outlawed; in the late 1500s in England, "gentlemen entering London had their swords measured and broken if they were too long for their status" (McCabe, 2015: 24). Depending on your interpretation, these laws were in place either to protect people from overspending on fads or to ensure that consumption was a visible marker of the existing social hierarchy (Shammas,

2012: 212). The justification for sumptuary laws often used the anti-consumption language of the "sin of luxury" and the economic dangers of "extravagance" (Hunt, 2003: 64). By the seventeenth century these laws gradually began to disappear. Although some types of consumption (for example, drugs and prostitution in many countries) are still outlawed, these restrictions are rarely designed to reinforce social hierarchies. A consumer society was not present before the 1700s for three reasons: consumers were a small minority, new items were not consistently generated, and consumerism was criticized as a moral failing because it ran counter to tradition (Stearns, 2001: 8–9).

Transformationists can make similar claims about the changes surrounding consumer credit. While credit has a very long history, the social attitudes about both lending and borrowing have changed drastically. Charging interest on loans – called usury – was frowned on by most religions. It was punishable by excommunication in the Catholic Church and is still forbidden in Islam. Judaism permitted charging interest to those from other religions, and so some Jews (who were often banned from other occupations) earned their income by lending money, a practice that was often viewed by Christians with considerable distaste. Christianity gradually relaxed its strict prohibitions so that usury came to mean charging unreasonably or immorally high interest rates (Wiedenhoft-Murphy, 2016). On the borrower side, although aristocrats would frequently go into debt using the collateral of their good name and the poor were often forced into debt to purchase staples, in the nineteenth century being a debtor was seen as a bit shameful (Stillerman, 2015). As we will discuss in chapter 3, the negative stigma of borrowing began to wane in the twentieth century, so that one might argue that, currently, it is completely acceptable never to be free of debt.

Others argue that the eighteenth-century transformation to the consumer society was driven not just by growing incomes and changed attitudes but also by a massive social and economic project. E. P. Thompson's classic "Time, Work-Discipline, and Industrial Capitalism" (1967) argues that, during the transition to industrialized, capitalist wage labour, employers and governments constantly complained of the lack of discipline, material ambition, punctuality and attendance by workers, who were accustomed to a more relaxed, less acquisitive lifestyle. The moral authority and socializing influence of organizations such as churches and schools had to be brought to bear to shame people out of "sloth," as they insisted on sleeping in when they were tired, taking customary holidays (such as "Saint Monday"), or knocking off early to go to the pub or to spend time with their children rather than keeping their noses to the grindstone to improve their material standing (Princen, 2005).

The second source of dispute revolves around whether consumption is driven by those who buy or those who make. Perhaps the most transparent title given to these two camps might be productivist and consumerist, although the more alliterative titles of "sucker" (productivist) and "savvy" (consumerist) might be more memorable (Paterson, 2017: 142–3). We will return to many versions of this argument in the rest of the book, but the general idea of the productivist camp is that both the income and the desire to consume are heavily influenced by the political economies that govern production. In the period between the seventeenth and the twentieth century, many European countries saw a transformation in the economic system from feudalism, in which the aristocracy ruled over its serfs in a largely agricultural system with joint rights for the use of land, to capitalism, in which land – along with all other inputs in production, except labour – is largely privately held.

Many productivists argue that this transformation revolutionized how people consume and the manner in which products are provided in several important ways. First, as much of the population shifted from having access to goods and services produced on their land, or in the broader non-market context of the feudal manor to which they belonged, to working for wage income, they relied much more on purchasing items from the market. The move between feudal agriculture and capitalist wage labour was not always voluntary or peaceful. In England, people were forced out of agriculture and into the wage labour market through the enclosure movements, which privatized common lands on which the feudal peasants relied as additional land for things such as raising livestock, making an agricultural livelihood almost impossible for many.

For productivists, the income that permits consumption is dependent on the amount and distribution of the spoils of the production process. While McKendrick et al. were correct in claiming that, in the eighteenth century, England was more affluent than other nations, it was also true that the limited national income and the uneven manner in which it was distributed meant that even in the nineteenth century many in that nation, especially those in the urban working class and in rural areas, earned so little that consumption activities, as we now know them, would have been a remote dream.

In the town of Preston in 1851, 52 percent of all working-class families with children below working age could not earn enough to rise above the poverty line even if they were employed full time for the year, which would have been a rarity (Hobsbawm, 1975: 221). Here is a description of the consumption of workers in England in 1844: "The potatoes which the workers buy are usually poor, the vegetables wilted, the cheese old and of poor quality, the bacon rancid, the meat lean, tough, taken from old, often diseased, cattle, or such as have died a natural death, and not fresh even then, often half decayed" (Engels, 1850: 68).

Competition for a customer base with very limited incomes coupled with a lack of government regulation over production practices resulted in serious quality issues for many products. A common practice at the time was to cut bread with sawdust as a cost-saving device. A study published in the medical journal *The Lancet* found that, in England during the 1850s, all of the bread, all the butter, half of the oatmeal, and just under half of the milk sampled were adulterated (Hobsbawm, 1964: 84–7).

Consumption is determined not only by income but also by prices, which are influenced by the system of production. The price reductions after the 1600s that were so important in the democratization of some long-distance goods – coffee, sugar and tobacco, for example – were the result of the despicable system of slave labour, which had a devastating long-term impact on the African countries from which slaves were captured (Nunn, 2008).

Further, according to the productivists, the desire for consumption is not independent of the process of production. People's wants and needs do not originate with themselves. Rather, consumers are manipulated into purchases that they would not have desired if not given a nudge by the seller. This is not a new phenomenon. As a widespread activity, advertising appeared in newspapers in the UK as early as the eighteenth century, but it has evolved and been considerably refined over time (Stillerman, 2015). As an article in the *Printers' Ink* journal in the 1920s approvingly noted, "advertising helps to keep the masses dissatisfied with their mode of life, discontented with ugly things around them. Satisfied customers are not as profitable as discontented ones" (Bonneuil and Fressoz, 2015: 155).

At the turn of the twentieth century, advertising was an unregulated wild west, where fantastical falsehoods were used to lure consumers (Dawson, 2003). This was especially common in health-improving products, which often advertised the curative properties of cocaine, laudanum and alcohol. To take one example, in 1905 Anheuser-Busch advertised Malt-Nutrine as a "scientific preparation of malt and hops" that "your physician will tell you ... will aid materially in the digestion and assimilation of food eaten. Dyspeptics, invalids and convalescents especially are benefited" (Figure 1.1).

Consumer rebellion against blatantly false claims, and the increased regulatory oversight of advertising that followed, changed the message but not the degree of manipulation, a topic to which we will return throughout the book. To provide just one example of how productivist scholars worry about the impact of more modern advertising, according to economist Juliet Schor's study of advertising to children at the turn of the 2000s, "by 18 months babies can recognize logos ... During their nursery-school years, children will request an average of 25 products a day ... children between the ages of six and twelve spend more time shopping than reading, attending youth groups, playing outdoors or spending time in household conversation" (quoted in Paterson, 2017: 211).

Finally, productivists often point out that what at first appear to be decisions around consumption may actually be decisions about production. In the early Industrial Revolution families increased their consumption of tobacco,

Figure 1.1 Anheuser-Busch advertisement, from *Theatre Magazine*, February 1905; www.bonkersinstitute.org/medshow/ buschtonic.html

tea, sugar and candles. This could be interpreted positively, as people having sufficient income for the consumption of life's little luxuries. Productivists, however, point out that all of these items were crucial to maintain energy and provide light to help poorly nourished workers toil incredibly long hours, many of which, especially for women, were in the home under the "putting-out system" that paid per unit produced (Trentmann, 2016). Some productivists also argue that consumption fills a void in people's lives created by the current system of production. Workers' inability to lead fulfilling work lives in the harsh, regimented, top-down control structures of wage labour led to consumption as an alternative sphere in which they could exercise control and express creativity (Bauman, 2008: 59–60). As the "sucker" nickname for consumers implies, it is probably also fair to say that the productivists are more pessimistic and critical of the role of consumption in society than the consumerists. Consumerists tend to view people as much more "savvy" in their consumption activities. This is not to deny that sellers frequently attempt to influence and manipulate their customers but to stress that the final decision in any act of consumption belongs to the consumer. Consumerists point to the fact that people consume in order to express their "own sense of identity" (Paterson, 2017: 143) through assemblages of commodities, cannily providing for their families, liberating themselves through transgressive displays, and engaging as savvy co-producers of brands. James Twitchell (1999), to whose writing we return in chapter 6, was an emblematic celebrant of this turn, casting it as a refreshing step away from the "scolding" tradition of productivists. Twitchell pointed out that increased consumption had expanded human welfare because it has genuine meaning, as people quest for affiliation, recognition and purpose. The power of the consumer is also shown when multinational firms bend their product offerings to local tastes rather than being able to alter tastes to meet their existing product offerings (Trentmann, 2009: 201–2). An obvious example of this might be that the champions of assembly-line food uniformity, McDonald's, introduced different menu items tailored for the tastes of different markets, producing the McVeggie in India and, much to the delight of those in the Eastern US, a McLobster during the summer months.

Consumerists also turn the table on the productivists by arguing that many revolutions in business and industry were actually driven by consumer demands. Rather than claiming, as the productivists do, that transformations in industry and trade led to the creation of products that had to find a place in consumer homes, consumerists argue that it was desire for more and novel products that created the impetus for industrialization (Trentmann, 2009: 196). For example, the expanded desire for porcelain, which had spread to the lower aristocracy and growing bourgeoisie, led to new production techniques pioneered by the English company Wedgwood (McKendrick et al., 1982). Many of the innovations in commerce and finance, such as the provision of credit and insurance, which was crucial in the time-consuming and uncertain business of long-distance trade, were caused by the demand for luxury consumption (Sassatelli, 2007: 23). More generally, consumerists argue that modern consumption preceded and provided impetus for the transformation of the economy toward industrial capitalism (Mukerji, 1983; Stillerman, 2015).

The consumerist and productivist positions are very different interpretations of who drives consumption and thus, often, the merits of a consumer society. For consumerists, consumption is driven by our genuine desire to use products in the process of "fashioning who we are" (Trentmann, 2016: 681). Productivists, on the other hand, argue that what we want, and whether we can have it, is driven by producers, creating real questions about whether we are better off at higher levels of consumption. This can sometimes appear a bit like the "chicken vs. egg" debate. Was it consumer demand for luxuries that led to the first long-distance trade, or was it the provision of luxuries from that trade that caused the demand for these products?

As with many of these types of debate, fence-sitters argue for a "multi-causal approach" in which both play a role in the rise of consumption and in driving consumer behaviour (Sassatelli, 2007: 13). This is the space occupied by writers such as Ben Fine, who argues that consumption takes place neither at the behest of a producer wielding the whip hand, nor in a realm of free expression and choice ruled by clear-eyed consumers, but in ways that compromise both. In Fine's view, while demand for commodified goods such as fashion is indeed generated and manipulated by producers seeking to increase sales, the strategies and successful campaigns to do so are in turn responsive to changing social currents, cultural shifts, and exogenously emergent demands (say, for "sweat-free" clothing or for the promotion of positive body-image) (Fine, 2002).

Contemporary sociology has also tried to reconcile the two sides of the consumption coin, most influentially through "practice theory," which focuses on how consumption fits into the things we do in our everyday lives (our "practices"). In Warde's (2017) formulation of the term, practices are the things we say and do, connected through understandings, know-how, descriptions, emotional states, motivations and rules. Practice theory is an attempt to allow for the intentionality and agency of consumers in how they interact with objects. They do so as part of finding meaning, satisfaction and sustenance through their day-to-day practices. At the same time, they do so under rules and constraints put in place partly by commercial interests who want us to buy stuff and partly by groups, organizations and other communities of practice (such as groups of cycling or motoring enthusiasts or gourmet cooks). We consume primarily not *as* a practice, in Warde's view, but almost always as part of our other practices – the purposeful, meaningful and expressive (building model trains, playing saxophone) as well as the unconscious everyday (heating our homes or taking a shower).

Practice theory does attend to the presence of commercial interest in the development of practices. But it also tends to reject arguments that are holistic – that connect practices to a set of "unified driving forces across the whole of the institutional complex" (Warde 2017: 170). Warde argues, for example, that, "even though producers try to mould our practices in line with their commercial interests, the practices are not dictated by producers of goods and services but rather directed by the symbolic and practical purposes that people pursue while going about their daily lives" (ibid.: 76–7). And so they are. But these purposes are equally open to conditioning not just by individual businesses who would like you to make Pepsi a part of your practice rather than Coke but by a systemic imperative that you live your life increasingly through the commodities it generates as a means of its self-expansion. It is in our commitment to a holistic explanation, rooted in an overarching, dominant system that governs the way we produce and reproduce our social existence, that our approach here deviates from practice theory, and it is in many ways a return to earlier forms of critique that do not shy from macro-scale analysis.

The commodity forms which, as Warde stresses, have colonized practices have done so as part of a political and cultural push to shape our means of going about our daily lives: to privatize and commodify them. To get at an explanation for consumption, we have to look at want, desire, meaning, purpose, and how these are developed in and through practices; but, in order to connect consumption to political economy, we have to situate this within a system whose logic is independent of these things, and possibly at odds with them.

The Rest of the Book

The rest of the book is dedicated to examining theories about how to interpret the modern world of capitalist commodity consumption. We will start with one consumerist theory that portrays consumption as an individual and beneficial decision. The subsequent chapter will critically evaluate this theory from a political economy perspective, with very different implications for the overall benefits of growing consumption and, therefore, the policy implications to remedy the identified shortcomings. The remaining chapters will examine the implications of individualized consumption for social well-being, for the environment, and for the distribution of power across classes and genders, and then look at the possibility of using consumerism as a political tool.

2

An Aspiration for All the World: Championing Individual Freedom of Choice

There is much cause to be grateful that ours is a consumer-oriented society.

(Katona, 1964: 4)

Introduction

You have just bought a fashionable shirt. Examining the many decisions that were made in purchasing that particular item as opposed to its many alternatives provides a useful, intuitive entry point into an analysis of consumption. The first decision might be whether to go out shopping for a shirt in the first place. With the money you spent on clothes you could have engaged in numerous other activities, from buying ice cream to enjoying a movie. Or you could have popped it in your savings account and relaxed in the park. The fact that you have opted for shirt purchasing would suggest that this was a more pressing desire than any of those alternatives.

Once you decided that the best use of your time and money was picking up a much needed top, you could then choose among a wide variety of alternative shirts from an impressive array of different stores or online vendors. In making that choice you would compare a number of different shirts – carefully looking at the cut, colour and fabric to choose the one that made you look your most presentable and feel the most comfortable. Additionally, you would consider how much hard-earned cash you wanted to part with. Was the slightly more flattering fit worth the extra money? In making each of these decisions you were most likely making the choice based on what you preferred. People don't often choose to go shopping for clothes if they have no food in the fridge. Nor do they usually select a shirt that they think looks terrible on them or is made of a scratchy, uncomfortable fabric. In their purchasing activities, people generally attempt to make choices that benefit them.

This may not seem like a particularly brilliant insight, but, at its core, this is the logic behind a theory that maintains that increasing household consumption should be the primary function of the economy and that, further, individual commodity consumption is the most efficient way to meet people's wide-ranging needs and desires. This chapter will lay out the intellectual history behind this justification, explore some of its implications, and examine some modifications of this theory that attempt to increase its "realism" while still maintaining its general policy conclusions.

From Classical to Neoclassical Economics: Consumers as Rational Maximizers

Adam Smith's *An Inquiry into the Nature and Causes of the Wealth of Nations* (Smith [1776] 1976) is often credited with being the first true work in economics, or what he would have called political economy. Smith's work was revolutionary in many ways, not the least of which was his insistence that consumption should be the primary purpose of production. Before Smith, self-interested consumption was commonly and negatively portrayed as greed, a base sentiment compared to "all the Virtue and Innocence that can be wish'd for in a Golden Age" (Mandeville, 1732). As we saw in chapter 1, certain types of consumption were even outlawed.

However, for Smith, consumption was nothing more than the pursuit of personal satisfaction and well-being (Sassatelli, 2010). Further, for Smith, the most effective manner in which consumption (and thus social welfare) could be maximized was through the invisible hand of the market guiding individual self-interest. For purchasers, this self-interest means getting the best product they can at the lowest cost. For firms, it is selling at the highest price. In this exchange of purchasers searching for bargains and firms searching for profits, a mutually agreeable deal can be struck that benefits both parties. "It is not from the benevolence of the butcher, the brewer, or the baker that we expect our dinner, but from their regard to their own interest. We address ourselves, not to their humanity but to their self-love, and never talk to them of our own necessities but of their advantages" (Smith, [1776] 1976: 18). Here we see Smith's transformation of what were previously considered to be vices into, if not quite virtues, at least necessary evils. For Smith, the efficient ability of the invisible hand to provide what society desired was dependent on consumers engaging in self-interested behaviour. The win–win agreement between parties with conflicting goals is possible because of competition. Sellers are likely to provide their customers with quality goods at reasonable prices because they know that unsatisfied buyers can move on to the seller's competitors.

As was generally true for his fellow classical economists, Smith argued there was a difference between the value at which goods are exchanged and the value that people place on goods in their use. This is expressed in the diamond–water paradox, in which Smith pointed out that people need water to live, resulting in a high use value. Yet the rate at which water can be traded for other goods – its exchange value or its price – was very low. Diamonds, on the other hand, had a very low use value compared to water, but a much higher exchange value (Smith [1776] 1976: 34). This paradox created a bit of a sticky contradiction because a good that was essential for life, and which people valued very highly in its use, had a much lower exchange value than a frivolous luxury. For the classical economists, exchange value was easy to measure by looking at the relative prices of two products, but it did not accurately represent the actual value to people. What did represent the actual value to people was particularly individual and, in the words of David Ricardo, "cannot be measured by any known standard" (cited in Stigler, 1950: 311).

The theory of consumption that emerged to dominate economics focused on the decisions of the purchaser and dismissed the difference between use and exchange value. The use–exchange issue was resolved by the neoclassicals by focusing on Jeremy Bentham's utilitarianism, in which "utility" depends on the pleasure or pain of an activity (Bentham, 1780). In this utilitarian view, there is no distinction between use and exchange value because, if something has a high exchange value, this must be true only because people gain a great deal of pleasure from it. It provides a foundation from which to say that whatever consumers buy is valuable and, conversely, that if there is no market demand for something, it must not be valuable. As University of Chicago economist George Stigler pointed out much later, "Smith's statement that value in use could be less than value in exchange was clearly a moral judgment, not shared by the possessors of diamonds" (Stigler, 1950: 308).

Three authors – William Jevons ([1871] 1957), Carl Menger ([1871] 2007) and Leon Walras (1954) – independently refined Bentham's model of a pleasure-seeking, pain-avoiding individual in a manner that won general acceptance in economics. While historians of economic thought are always careful to point out that there were important differences between these three writers, it was what they had in common that created the foundations for the neoclassical theory of consumption. This theory, in which consumers take center stage by sending out signals to which firms respond, is based on a series of assumptions about how people behave and the appropriate level of analysis for the economic discipline. In terms of assumptions about behaviour, people are understood as rational utility maximizers. This means that they have the ability and motivation to understand the utility they receive from their consumption activities, weigh them against the prices being charged, and compare them across purchases in order to generate the maximum utility possible from their consumption budget. People are also assumed to be insatiable – to believe that more is always better, or at least never worse. This does not necessarily mean that they try to consume as many products as possible, but they do attempt to maximize their utility from pleasure-producing consumption while minimizing the amount of pain-producing work effort (we will ignore, for the moment, the potentially problematic double insistence that work is a source of pain while pleasure comes from purchases, which we will take up in chapter 3). This theory also assumes that people's utility is individualistic in that it stems from their own intrinsic personal benefit from consumption rather than being influenced by others. How those preferences are formed to create choices of one product over another, or between leisure and consumption, is not really the subject of inquiry. The social, cultural and economic institutions that might affect consumption are not examined by economics, although they might, perhaps, be the legitimate subject of another discipline (Ackerman, 1997: 651). For neoclassical economists such as Gary Becker, these non-economic disciplines can contribute best to social science by figuring out how preferences form, in order that they might be plugged into what he called the "economic approach" in which "all human behavior can be viewed as involving participants who maximize their utility from a stable set of preferences and accumulate an optimal amount of information and other inputs in a variety of markets" (Becker, 1976: 14).

Like Smith, the neoclassical writers put some thought into how the products from which households can choose would be distributed among the population. Walras produced a theory of general equilibrium in which he demonstrated that a competitive market could produce the type and quantity of products that would yield the maximum possible utility for households (Stigler, 1950: 322). "Production in a market governed by free competition is an operation by which the [productive] services may be combined in products of appropriate kind and quantity to give the greatest possible satisfaction of needs" (Walras, 1954: 231). Despite Walras's claims that his theory was an important step in moving economics in the direction of a pure science, and that it did not contain moral judgements (Hunt, 1979: 267), this was patently not the case, since, like Smith's, his theory contained the very strong implication that an economy organized as a competitive market would distribute goods among households in a manner that would ensure the most utility. Maximizing the total utility of all members of society is a controversial goal with important moral judgements.

Perhaps most obviously, maximizing total utility ignores its distribution between people. If income were redistributed so that it increased the utility of the very rich and decreased the utility of the very poor, this would represent a social improvement as long as the increase for the rich was greater than the decrease for the poor.

Alternative goals which explicitly acknowledge the importance of how income is distributed have been put forward, from egalitarianism to Rawlsian justice (which seeks to ensure a respectable income for the poorest members of society). Notwithstanding these pesky inconveniences to what the neoclassicals viewed as their purely scientific theory of the economy, it was nonetheless true that, as one economic historian put it, Jevons, Menger and Walras opened up a theory of consumption in which individual behaviour should be modelled as "rational, calculating maximization of utility" (Hunt, 1979: 237). These foundations have been further formalized and refined by subsequent authors, particularly Alfred Marshall, who measured the utility of commodities in terms of the price at which they exchanged and argued that the utility of individuals could be added together to measure the utility of all products (Stigler, 1950: 326). "We may regard the aggregate of the money measures of the total utility of wealth as a fair measure of that part of happiness which is dependent on wealth" (Marshall, 1890: 179–80). In other words, the amount of money you spend on a shirt is a direct measure of how much happiness you get out of it. Add up all the spending on shirts, pants, socks, Xboxes, Teslas and the rest, and you get a pretty solid assessment of happiness from all purchased consumption in society. You might also get some joy from picking daisies in a field, but economics hasn't paid much attention to daisy-picking (at least it didn't until the economics of happiness emerged and discovered that much of what makes us happy cannot be purchased).

Some of the proponents of the rational maximizing consumer are not completely convinced that it represents an accurate assumption of how people behave. Yet they argue that, despite its lack of realism, it should still be maintained. This point was perhaps most famously made by Milton Friedman (1953), who argued that theories should be judged not on their descriptive accuracy but whether their predictions are successful. So it may not be true that people are actually capable of the complex calculus of genuine rational maximizing, but, because the predictions that follow from assuming that people behave in this manner are accurate, the theory should be judged favourably. Friedman uses the example of a billiards player to illustrate his point. Billiards players do not actually make all the complicated geometrical calculations in preparing a shot. However, if you modelled players "as if" they made these calculations, it would most likely provide a fairly good prediction of the shot that they would actually make. Similarly, consumers may not go through the mental gymnastics required to calculate the utility from different purchases, but if the predictions that stem from modelling consumers "as if" they do yield accurate predictions, then that is a sound basis to accept this assumption.

This particular species of consumer, based as it is on some fairly strong assumptions about human nature, was deemed a sufficiently unique animal that it merited its own scientific name – Homo oeconomicus. Consumers were modelled as (if not actually thought to be) actors capable of making rational choices in order to gain maximum satisfaction from their buying (Sassatelli, 2010). As we shall see, not all economists were convinced that this species actually existed, but it was sufficiently entrenched as a model of the individual that one observer in the mid-1990s could declare: "I suspect that the majority of economists remain confident of the survival of their favorite species. In fact, many see economic man as virtually the only civilized species" (Persky, 1995).

Even in economics, the characterization of consumers as insatiable individuals, interested in, and capable of, maximizing utility, had its critics. As we shall see in chapter 4, those critics have become more numerous in recent decades. Other academic disciplines have been even more scathing in their rejection. Sociologist Pierre Bourdieu, for example, referred to Homo oeconomicus as a "kind of anthropological monster. ... the most extreme personification of the scholastic fallacy," an error "by which the scholar puts into the heads of the agents he is studying ... the theoretical considerations and constructions he has had to develop in order to account for those practices" (Bourdieu [1988] 2016: 209). In subsequent chapters of this book, we will examine many of the theories from other disciplines, particularly sociology, which reject Homo oeconomicus and embed consumption in a broader context. However, despite the academic scorn heaped on Homo oeconomicus, it provides a compelling justification for the "consumerist" interpretation. First, people know what creates satisfaction for them, and this cannot be judged by any outside observer. The act of paying for diamonds or Instagram-inspired clothing indicates that these items yield genuine satisfaction for the buyer. Further, the amount paid represents a measure of how much utility the consumer receives from the purchase. Consumers are also capable of judging the benefits they receive from alternative products, whether that is different offerings within the same category (for example, a Hyundai versus a Ford) or different categories of products (a car versus a vacation). This theory of the consumer lends itself to the idea that consumers know what is best for them and will be well served by a policy environment in which they can exercise their freedom of choice. It importantly also provides a justification for increasing consumption being interpreted as increasing individual well-being and, therefore, an important social goal. The model of Homo oeconomicus provides a logic for the dominant discourse surrounding the sovereignty of the consumer and the pre-eminence of consumer choice.

To see one example of how these premises justify the benefits of consumer choice and dismiss government intervention in consumption, we can look at Friedman's example of consumer safety – whether the things people consume are safe. For Friedman, the combination of rational, self-interested consumers and a competitive market rendered regulations unnecessary. Since people take advantage of the information available to them, indeed, even seek out information on products, any substandard or hazardous products are likely to be detected by savvy consumers and the miscreant firms punished as customers reject their inferior or dangerous goods. Using Friedman's own rhetorical flourish, the answer to the question "Who protects the consumer?" is "other firms" (Friedman, 1962), but this is possible only if people are well informed and rational.

A controversial example of this is Friedman's claim that "licensure has reduced both the quantity and quality of medical practice" (Friedman, 1962: 158). According to Friedman, there should be no rules specifying the amount and type of training for health professionals. Providers of medical services will offer appropriate and affordable treatments in the absence of mandated training because consumers, able to discern effective treatments from chicanery, will demand it of them. Further, any practitioner that does provide poor service will soon find themselves out of business courtesy of market competition. "Insofar as [the doctor] harms only his patient, that is simply a question of voluntary contract and exchange between patient and physician. On this score, there is no ground for intervention" (ibid.: 147). Anyone with the inclination and ability should be able to hang out a medical shingle and the well-informed consumer will ensure that the market separates the healer from the quack.

In a more positive manner, freedom of choice is also held to be an important principle in its own right. It is an important principle of liberalism, which puts forward an idea of liberty that is based on maximizing the scope of choice that does not reduce the liberties of another. For liberals, government intervention reduces liberty by restricting the freedom to engage in voluntary and, consequently, mutually improving exchanges. For example, policies that would tax, restrict or ban the sale of high-sugar drinks have been criticized on the basis that these dietary choices are best left to the individual and that government has no role interfering with the free choice of consumers. While an "unfettered" consumer is not, strictly speaking, necessary to liberal theory, the claim that people are rational maximizers, capable of making decisions that are genuinely welfare improving, lends credence to the idea that people should be free to make their own consumption choices.

Friendly Amendments: Alterations to the Theory with Similar Implications

Like the Yeti, Homo oeconomicus is very difficult to find in the field. Critics have expressed varying degrees of doubt over the ability of individual, rational, maximizing assumptions to predict accurately how consumers actually behave. In this section we will focus on some modifications to these assumptions which still maintain the positive normative implications about consumption in our society.

Joseph Schumpeter broke from the neoclassical economists on a number of fronts, perhaps most famously their focus on static efficiency, analyzing economic performance at any one moment in time. In terms of consumption, static efficiency would mean that the largest quantity of a good should be produced at the lowest price – a result that would occur when supply equaled demand in a competitive marketplace. Schumpeter argued that thinking about a capitalist economy at any specific moment in time is to miss the point of the entire economic system, which is the dynamic "creative destruction" of the old by the new (Schumpeter, [1943] 2010: 73). This dynamism is at its best, according to Schumpeter, when facilitated by high prices and industries dominated by a few large concerns, which create the income and incentive for investment and innovation (ibid.: 79).

Schumpeter's general idea of creative destruction creates a picture of the consumer that, in some ways, contrasts with the neoclassical picture of rational, individual maximization. The main distinction is that, in Schumpeter's economy of continuous creation and destruction of products, consumers will not have a complete understanding of the menu of options available to them. New products and options will always be cropping up with which people have no experience and, therefore, will have difficulty evaluating. As a result, their tastes and preferences are not properly formed and not perfectly understood. In the absence of personal familiarity, people's preferences are influenced by their social environment, and especially by innovative consumers who eagerly try, evaluate and publicize new products, blazing a trail for others to follow (Jonsson, 1994: 309). People rely heavily on custom and experience to make their decisions on goods with which they are familiar, creating an inertia that must be broken in order for people to change their preferences.

This is a different consumer than that modelled by the neoclassicals. Rather than being able to maximize utility from the consumption of products, people fumble haltingly toward their desired spending patterns. Further, unlike the neoclassicals, Schumpeter argued that people's preferences are malleable rather than individually determined and that an important area of economic inquiry should be the manner in which preferences are formed (Jonsson, 1994: 307). However, Schumpeter's differences from the neoclassicals over consumer behaviour must be placed in the overarching context of his overwhelmingly positive interpretation of innovation in consumer goods. For Schumpeter, the genius of capitalism was not ensuring low prices through competition but its tremendous capacity to better the human condition through new products and techniques of production. Consumers may not be rational maximizers in the neoclassical sense, but they most definitely benefit from the new technologies made available by the process of creative destruction.

One group did follow up on Schumpeter's desire to study some of the influences on consumer preferences. These "behaviouralists" were uncomfortable with the lack of similarity between Homo oeconomicus and what psychological research has established about how humans actually behave. An early pioneer in this area was George Katona. He was particularly concerned that consumers' desires and motivations were being overly simplified by the neoclassical economic assumptions and sought to discover what people were actually up to in their purchasing behaviour (Caplovitz, 1966). Based on his analysis of extensive consumer surveys, Katona deduced that, although consumers did attempt to inform themselves on economic matters, they were often slow to learn, which did not square well with the assumption of rational maximization (Hosseini, 2017: 132). Habitual behaviour and genuine decision-making were, according to Katona, the two most common determinants of purchasing behaviour. "The American consumer is a sensible person and is a discriminating buyer who seeks information and tries to understand what is going on. ... This does not mean that he is an ideal rational man. Old stereotypes and attitudes persist even when no longer applicable and habitual behavior is very common" (Katona, 1964: 333). While individuals may not be rationally maximizing in the genuine neoclassical sense, they are sufficiently well informed to understand their desires and are able to realize them through their purchasing behaviour.

The manner in which Katona interprets the role of advertising in society is a good example of how he viewed consumption. For Katona, advertising does not sway impressionable consumers into frivolous purchases. Rather, it plays a vital role in informing people about a product's existence, function and price. Further, to the extent that a few commercials do attempt to sway people's purchasing through "unreasoned appeals" which rely on emotion rather than fact, these are likely to work only for unimportant goods, such as toothpaste, on which people will not expend a great deal of time and effort in making their decisions (Katona, 1964: 58–9). The individual is "not a pawn moved about by marketers and advertisers at will" (ibid.: 333). Katona does reject that idea that people have individually determined "autonomous" preferences. He argues that people's desires are primarily influenced not by the allure of marketing but by groups to which they belong, such as their family or friends. Like Schumpeter, Katona maintains that, because of product innovation, consumers do not really understand the full range of choices available to them. Many valuable products, from air conditioning, to automobiles, to cigarettes, were not originally wanted by consumers, but, once they were created and popularized, these products were successful only because they satisfied a genuine desire from consumers (ibid.: 55).

Katona's normative conclusions about the role of consumption in society portrayed the growing mass consumption of the early 1960s in an overwhelmingly positive light. According to Katona, the neoclassical assumption of non-satiation was backed up by his survey data. The more people have, the more they want. As we shall see in later chapters, some critics of consumerism place a negative spin on this for a variety of reasons, but Katona argued that these growing aspirations are beneficial for the individual and the economy.

For the individual, the continued desire for materialistic consumption is the hallmark of a flourishing society in which the masses can obtain what, in the past, would have been the exclusive domain of the rich (Katona, 1960). "The common man can have what he likes rather than what he needs" (Katona, 1964: 4). For the economy, increased material aspiration is what encourages people to work hard, creating economic growth. "It is precisely the wanting and striving for improvement in private living standards that forms the solid basis for American prosperity" (ibid.: 65). Far from being wasteful consumption, this represents the triumph of a successful economy: "by raising the living standards of the American masses and demonstrating to the world at large that it is possible for the greater majority of the people to live decently, the United States has once against presented new goals and aspirations for all the world" (ibid.: 53).

Another slight modification of neoclassical theory stressed that consumers' utility comes from the characteristics that goods offer rather than the goods themselves (Ackerman, 1997: 659). To use an example from K. J. Lancaster (1966), all dish detergents are not equal. They contain a bundle of different characteristics that consumers may find more or less appealing, from their cleaning ability to their scent. If the characteristics of the dish soap are altered, for example, by adding a skin softener, then it should not be considered to be the same good, providing the same utility to consumers as a detergent that leaves your hands dry and chapped. Here, again, advertising plays an important and positive role for consumers. Given the complex collection of characteristics embodied in any good, providing consumers with information on the diverse and beneficial "consumption technology" available to them fulfills an important social function. As with Katona, the role of advertising illustrates Lancaster's general interpretation of consumption, which is that people's choice between characteristics leads to maximizing their utility.

So, for Katona, Lancaster and Schumpeter, people are well served by an economy geared toward innovating new consumer products. For Lancaster, the inclusion of new features in a product actually changed the product, and if consumers approved of the new characteristic it would represent an increase in satisfaction from the same good or service. For Katona, the desire for more and more up-to-date consumer goods was not only good for those who had the wherewithal to purchase them, but it also provided a beacon of possibility and motivation for those who could not. Consumption beyond need, once associated with pride, vanity and wastefulness, became a virtue.

However, for Katona and for Schumpeter, against the grain of neoclassical conceptions, consumers' preferences – only half-informed at best, in flux and socially conditioned – did not operate as the sole signal for what is to be produced in society. Entrepreneurs could tap into desires that were latent or unrealized, capitalizing on the plasticity of want. It was this latter group that provided the dynamism of capitalism, in Schumpeter's view, and if consumers had to sacrifice in the short term by paying high prices in uncompetitive markets, they would reap the rewards in the long term with newer, better and even unheard of products.

Conclusion

This chapter examined the theories that put the best possible spin on shirt purchasing and the rest of our consumption activities. When we buy a shirt, it is because we want it more than other things that we could spend our money on. As put forward so long ago by Adam Smith, when we buy a shirt we enter into a voluntary trade with the seller that appeals to both parties' self-interest. Consumers would only accept the trade if it improved their well-being. In making the exchange, the buyer is implicitly acknowledging that the shirt is worth more than the money for which it was exchanged. In this sense, no market-based consumption can be done without the consumer's consent. The neoclassical introduction of rational, individual maximization implies that, in choosing the shirt, we are able rationally to weigh our options about what else we could have done with the money, from buying something completely different, such as a dinner out, to purchasing a shirt of a slightly different style and colour. This idea is as true for something as important as health care as it is for something arguably less life changing, such as a shirt.

This does not mean that everyone will be happy. Rather, it suggests that we have chosen the shirt because it is the best thing we could have purchased given our choices of products, our preferences and our income. As we shall see in some subsequent chapters, there is nothing inevitable about the link between individual rational maximization and the claim that commodity consumption is beneficial for the buyer.

However, some economists, such as Friedman, have used the idea of well-informed consumer choice in competitive markets to argue that market competition delivers whatever the consumer wants at the best price. It is also true that it is not completely necessary to assume an individual rational maximizing human to arrive at the conclusion that people are well served by consumption activities. As the theories of Schumpeter, Lancaster and Katona indicate, it is possible for firms to drive consumption and inform consumers, pushing people to try new things and develop new tastes. Yet, even in this situation, in which firms take the lead in the consumption–production dance, they only succeed if their new products tap into a previously unknown consumer desire. In the savvy vs. sucker distinction introduced in chapter 1, the authors here are firmly in the savvy camp. In the next chapter we will introduce a theory of political economy that places these market activities explicitly in the economic system in which they take place, which creates very different conclusions about the extent to which consumers are savvy or suckers.

3
The System: Capitalist Consumerism

Introduction

Why were your clothes made? In 2018, talk-show host, comedian and LGBTQ advocate Ellen DeGeneris claimed the "biggest inspiration [for her EV1 clothing line in partnership with Walmart] was actually inclusiveness" (quoted in Thomas, 2018). When discussing her desire to create a new line of children's clothing, rapper and TV personality Cardi B lamented the current sartorial offerings: "I want to be able to design what I want for my daughter to wear" (quoted in Magsaysay, 2018). DeGeneris's answer would suggest that her collection was made so that a wider range of people can be fashionable. Cardi B's motivation appears to be a combination of a creative outlet for herself and a desire to provide a few clothing options for her assumedly underserved daughter. These two entrepreneurs are no exception. When firms are asked why they do whatever they do, whether it's making cell phones or T-shirts, the answer is usually about their passion for the product and desire to improve people's lives.

While these answers aren't lies – and we would not want to cast any suspicion on DeGeneris's or Cardi B's motivations – this is not really why your clothes (or cars or cell phones) are made. In capitalism, firms produce things to turn a profit. This does not necessarily mean that all other motives are irrelevant, rather that they are instrumental. If they help firms make money, they will be encouraged. If they hinder profitability, they will be dropped. In fact, when answering most questions about production today, whether it's why clothes are made, why they are made in a particular way, or why they are sold to certain customers, the best answer is usually, "it makes the most money."

Capitalist Commodity Production: Naming the System

A political economy of modern consumption takes as its starting point that consumption is conditioned by the logic of the capitalist system in which most of it occurs. In the analysis of consumption and capitalism that follows, we take many of our cues from Karl Marx's description of capitalism and the categories he used to critique it. Consumption did exist in other economic systems, such as slavery and feudalism, but the logic through which consumption items are produced and the conditions under which people consume differ between systems. In capitalism most consumption goods are commodities that are sold with the express intent of making a profit. Further, for firms in a competitive capitalist system, the profit must be reinvested in ways that will generate profits in the future (anything from developing new products or new production techniques to lobbying to avoid costly regulation), creating a circuit of investment, production, sales and reinvestment. The motivation of commodity production governs, although does not necessarily determine, the manner in which people consume in our society (Fine, 2002).

Marxist-influenced theories of consumption have been subject to critiques. They are most prominently charged with framing consumption as an "animal function" (Marx, 1977: 66) (thus ignoring its meaningful, communicative and relational nature) (Paterson, 2017: 15). However, a Marxist approach need not do this, and it usefully highlights two aspects that are crucial for the political economy of consumption. One is the emphasis on class conflict. The other is to stress that consumption – no matter its variety, the agency and savvy of consumers, its unevenness across race and gender – is conditioned significantly by production, including the imperatives of profitability and growth (or "accumulation") made central by Marx. How we behave as consumers is not independent of the needs and efforts of producers, as these are subject in turn to capitalism's laws of motion. Capitalism is a class system, with frequently conflicting interests between different classes. One crucial conflict is between those that own the productive capacity and those who work for them. This is the famed division between workers and owners. However, in terms of consumption, another conflict worth noting is between firms (or, more exactly, between the people who own and control firms), which produce products that they need to sell, and households, who need to buy.

Like poorly costumed superheroes, most people in capitalism lead a dual life as workers and customers. Firms depend on people (other than the firms' owners) for their profits in two very different ways. First, in the process of production, workers generate profits by being paid less than the value of what they produce. The intuition behind this is that, if a worker creates $70,000 worth of value for a company, the company can only pay the worker something less than $70,000. If the company paid the worker more it would be losing money by hiring that worker, which will ensure a very short life for the firm. The closer workers can get to earning the value of what they produce, the smaller the profit a company makes on its hiring practices. This creates one of many obvious conflicts between workers and firms. The difference between the value that employees produce and the wages they get paid is called surplus value.

Firms also need people to buy their products in order for this surplus value, created in the production process, to be realized as actual profits. Once a car is built, the value embedded in it will remain unrealized while it sits on the factory lot. It is only once it is sold that it is converted into profit. It is here that households play their second crucial role, buying things so that surplus value can be realized as profit. The realization of surplus value creates conflicts between firms and households. It is not doing a horrible injustice to the calculation of the firm to say that, the more it can induce people to buy and the higher the price at which it can sell, the greater its realization of profits. Just to take one of these as an example, firms' profits are increased the faster their products can be used up or destroyed (Dawson, 2003). For a shampoo manufacturer, it is far better if people rinse and repeat than merely rinse. Household motivations in consumption are a little more complex. Michael Dawson, not unlike "practice theorists," argues that the goal of people is to use products for the "sustenance and enjoyment of life" (ibid.: 5). As ambiguous as this goal is, it suggests some obvious conflicts with firms. The shampoo example illustrates the general idea that people would like products to have a long, useful life, which runs counter to the firms' desire to sell products. Other less trivial examples abound. In 2018, the Italian government fined Apple and Samsung €10 million and €5 million respectively for deliberately sabotaging the performance of older models of their phones through operating system updates that "caused serious malfunctions and significantly reduced performance, thus accelerating phones' substitution" (Gibbs, 2018).

According to some political economists, a fundamental part of the conflict between buyer and seller is over how, or whether, consumption contributes use value (Fine, 2002: 28). According to German philosopher Wolfgang Haug, people's goal in a commodity exchange is to satisfy a want. The commodity's ability to satisfy that want is its "use value" to the consumer. The seller is attempting to realize an exchange value by appealing to the use value of the good to the purchaser (Haug, 1986: 15). Haug coined the term "commodity aestheticism" to get at the overarching role of commodity characteristics, from design to marketing, in acting as "bait" to entice consumers by appealing to, and creating, needs (ibid.:17). This bait is effective only to the extent that it can appeal to the actual wants of the purchaser, and so "the commodity is created in the image of the consumer's desires" (ibid.: 24). Sut Jhally argues that the use value of almost all products, even the most basic, is made up of a combination of culturally defined functionality and culturally based interpretation of meaning. The role of advertising is not to separate meaning from function, since this is impossible, but to create meaning for a product. The creation of commodities in capitalism hides their meaning (this will be elaborated further in the "Commodity Fetishism" section that follows). It is advertising that creates it, although this intended meaning is mediated and interpreted by advertising's targets (Jhally, 1987). Returning again to the diamond example, the fact that a rock is culturally valued as a symbol of status and love must, in some part, be down to the efforts of DeBeers (which had a virtual monopoly on the diamond market until the 2000s) and its jewelry retailers to convince people that, in the words of a DeBeer's marketing campaign, "a diamond is forever" (more on this in chapter 4).

There is an important contrast to be made between the political economy of consumption theorized in this chapter and Schumpeter's idea of creative destruction from chapter 2. In both theories, firms are providing people with products that they do not already want and have to be convinced to buy. However, the theory in this chapter suggests that the world is littered with innovations of more dubious benefit than Schumpeter's creative destruction would imply. For every smartphone there is a cigarette (and those whose children are screen-addicted may feel the smartphone's alleged benefits are by no means a settled matter). Equally, marketing is often not for new products but for those with which people are well acquainted. People do not need to be introduced to diamonds, but they must be constantly reminded of their value.

It is not only the theory of consumption put forward in this chapter that acknowledges the conflicting interests of consumer and producer. Adam Smith's invisible hand was based on self-interested sellers wanting to charge the highest price and buyers wanting to pay the lowest. For Smith, and those who follow in his market-advocating footsteps in chapter 2, the conflict of interest is resolved when buyers and sellers settle on a mutually agreeable price through voluntary exchange, which ensures that every transaction improves the well-being of both consumers and producers.

Although market exchange in capitalism is indeed voluntary, it occurs within power relationships that are not necessarily beneficial for the buyer. The power of the buyer is that they are the final arbiters of what is, and what is not, produced through their right of refusal – their ability to vote with their money. Generally speaking, the power of the firm in this relationship is grounded in its ability to manipulate people's consumer choices and behaviours (Dawson, 2003). While the ability of firms to manipulate consumers, and the manner in which they do so, has changed with the historical period (a point we will take up in the final section of this chapter), the power of the large modern corporation rests on its detailed knowledge about their customers and its effective ways of channelling people's off-the-job activities into profit-enhancing consumption. How to coerce consumers has always been a profitable avenue of inquiry for firms – from training sales staff in the appropriate manner to elicit sales from different types of customers to focus groups that discover what types of beer labels are most likely to attract the eye favourably. In fact, households have been endlessly studied by firms with an eye for any possibility of decreasing costs or increasing sales. The business model of Google and Facebook, in which people's online data are used to predict consumer behaviour and preferences and to target advertisements, is only a current evolution of this longstanding practice.

Whether the capitalist system of commodity production serves people or firms in the realm of consumption is dependent on the balance of power between these two groups (Dawson, 2003). People's ability to vote with their money means that companies do not have a free hand to produce goods and services that people do not want. Automobile firms could not produce a car that needed to be replaced every month – unless it was really cheap. It is easy to point to examples, such as the manufacturer of Blackberry phones, of companies that went into sharp decline because they could not attract customers. On the other hand, any discussion of preferences must acknowledge that firms have considerable ability to influence consumers. What is produced in a capitalist system is what will be profitable, and realizing profits cannot be left to the undirected discretion of the consuming public.

In the conflict between firm and consumer, the power wielded by each is not an unalterable condition of the political economy of capitalism. Within the dictates of private, for-profit commodity production, the rules of communication between consumer and producer can tilt the balance of power in favour of one group or another. A very small recent example of this that favoured buyers occurred when product endorsements on social media in the United States were forced to be transparently labelled as sponsored content. A more significant example involves advertising to children. Allowing firms a free hand to market to children aids profit realization in a manner that harms households in obvious, nag-increasing ways. As a result, some jurisdictions have placed limits on the manner in which firms can communicate to children. For example, in 2006 the UK banned advertising for unhealthy foods (high in fat, sugar or sodium) on children's TV programs. In 1992 Norway outlawed TV advertising aimed at children under sixteen.

Of course, because these rules alter the power relationships in consumption, they too will be the subject of conflict in the political system. Conceivably, remarkably wide-ranging rule changes could dramatically reduce the power of firms to use commodity aestheticism as bait. For example, rather than being a venue for eye-catching allure, packaging could simply be a space to inform consumers – as when Canadian cigarette packages show their contents' effects on your lungs. Public space dedicated to corporate messaging, from billboards to online advertising, could be limited. Non-informational advertising could be banned. None of these things are currently being seriously considered, which helps create a favourable atmosphere for the influence of firms over customers.

The conflict between firms and consumers isn't just about getting you to pick a Samsung over an Apple. It is also about generating a default assumption that wants and desires are best satisfied through commodity consumption and that choice over commodities is a fundamental aspect of freedom. Herbert Marcuse famously distilled the essence of advanced industrial society to an *illusion* of liberty in the form of choice. "Free choice among a wide variety of goods and services," he argued, "does not signify freedom if these goods and services sustain social controls over a life of toil and fear – that is, if they sustain alienation" (Marcuse, [1964] 1991: 6–7). Our consumerism, in other words, keeps us happy, but in chains nonetheless. We return to Marcuse's claims on this front in chapter 6.

The conflict is also over the quantity and value of the commodities seen as necessary to satisfy any given need.

Most of the items in a North American garage, from yard tools to outdoor games, lie dormant most of the time. All of these might just as easily be cooperatively owned by a group of neighbours with little loss of satisfaction, and maybe even some increase (less clutter, more neighbourly interaction). We already do meet some of our most important needs – K-12 education, parks, sports fields and subways – through non-commodified, public means. The possibilities of communal or public, rather than private, ownership of the "means of enjoyment" are enormous. We also, of course, seek enjoyment through taking a stroll, talking with friends, or jumping off a rock into a river. These sometimes require some things to go along with the activity, but usually a bare minimum.

Businesses, however, lose out on this. In order to profit, they need our consumption, so public, cooperative or other forms of non-commodified need satisfaction represent obstacles to be overcome. A low-hanging example is yoga – whose teachings promote simplicity and whose practice could be accomplished with nothing but your body and the ground – but which now generates $80 billion in global sales (Delaney, 2017), as firms convince people that their true path to spiritualism and wellness is via the right kind of pants. Investment and social resources under capitalism flow to what is expected to deliver the most profit. Sometimes this overlaps with creating the most enjoyment for people, but, as we'll see, there are plenty of occasions when they do not. The conflict, then, is not just over better or worse, cheaper or more tasteful products, but over the whole question of how we will meet our needs for survival and for enjoyment.

Commodity Fetishism

Another concept introduced by Karl Marx, what he called "commodity fetishism," sheds further light on this conflict. The concept contains within it an account of the complex relationships between substance and appearance in commodity production and exchange (see Hudson and Hudson, 2003). For our purposes, though, two aspects are key. Marx pointed out that commodities, while they seem straightforward, are actually mysterious, magical objects. Both the magic and the mystery are important. Let's begin with the magic. A "fetish" is (in one sense of the word) an object imbued with powers – something that will provide aid and support to its possessor. So one aspect of commodity fetishism is that, in a consumer society, we seek out qualities and characteristics through what Marx would term the "alienated" form of the commodity. Vehicles, clothing, food, razors, appliances, shoes and home accessories are imbued with the power to convey qualities and states on their possessors: attractiveness, freedom, cosmopolitanism, athleticism, security, love. We, in turn, seek to capture and express these qualities and achieve these states through the ownership of commodities rather than through other means.

The flipside of the "phantom qualities" we see in commodities is the great difficulty we have seeing or recognizing the actual labour (or the transformation of nature; Fine, 2002: 26) that brings commodities into being. This is where the mystery comes in, and it gives a considerable edge to sellers in the consumption conflict. When you are purchasing your shirt, as we'll see in chapter 5, the appearance of the object – soft fabric, bright colours, attractive cut – tells you nothing about the labour and parts of nature that are embodied in it. Since we discuss environmental transformations in chapter 5, it is enough to say here that, in looking at one shirt or another, we have no immediate knowledge of whether the labour that brought it into existence was that of an indentured minor working under conditions of modern slavery, a team of unionized workers in a garment factory, or a single skilled tailor operating out of their own shop. There are ways that producers try to signal this, as we'll see in chapter 7, but the nature of the commodity is to obscure these relations. While shoppers may have strongly held preferences about working conditions or about environmental degradation, knowledge of these things is hard to come by, hidden beneath the appealing "material shell" (Marx, [1867] 1976: 167, n. 29) of fruit, fish, fashion and furniture that consumers encounter.

Consumption and Jobs

Profits depend on people continuing their consuming ways, but it is not only firms that benefit from consumption. In a capitalist economy, profits also influence how much firms will invest (therefore, also how much technology and of what kind will be adopted) and whether they are likely to employ more people. The idea that demand drives the overall economy is probably best associated with economist J. M. Keynes and his post-Keynesian (PK) followers.

Writing in the 1930s, Keynes argued that the decade-long economic collapse of the Great Depression was caused by a decline in demand, which started a vicious cycle in which reductions in sales led to reductions in jobs, which in turn led to further declines in demand, sales and employment. Keynes's revolutionary solution was for government to step in and shore up demand through such policies as providing public-sector employment and increasing wages (Keynes, 1936). Keynesian demand management became common policy practice when the massive increase in government-funded military spending for World War II was seen as the decisive factor in ending the Great Depression in North America.

Consumption is only one part of demand, which in this context is a desire to buy by any actor in the economy – so it also includes government spending, investment by firms (in real things as opposed to just paper investment such as buying stocks) and net exports purchased by foreigners. However, consumption is a crucial component of overall demand and is much more stable than investment, which Keynes argued was subject to unpredictable changes in business confidence that he termed "animal spirits." In PK theory, increased demand, of which consumption is a crucial part, will be met by increased production by firms, which in turn increases the amount of employment (Davidson, 2015). For most PK theorists, unemployment is a great failing of the economy, representing a waste of social resources and a considerable cost to the individual worker, which should be avoided by increasing demand.

One particular variant of PK, associated with Michal Kalecki, stresses the role of income *distribution* in increasing demand (Kalecki, 1943, 1971). Kalecki argues that workers, who have modest earnings, consume more and save less per dollar of income than wealthier owners. It follows that channelling income to workers and away from owners will create greater demand. However, in most economies, the income of owners is sufficiently large that it constrains demand below levels that would create full employment. The implication is that redistributing income from rich to poor (or owners to workers) would not only create more equality but boost current demand and, therefore, employment. Ironically, increasing workers' pay might even increase profits despite increasing the firm's costs, because it would increase demand.

In PK theory, deficient demand is not only an immediate problem because it reduces output and employment. It also decreases investment, which is a problem for future growth. In PK theory, the animal spirits of investors are influenced by expectations of future profits, formed at least in part by recent past profits, which are in turn dependent on the demand for firms' products. This creates a relationship between current demand and the purchase of capital goods and new technology, which determines future economic prospects (Kalecki, 1971; King, 2008).

The importance of demand in both current and future economic prosperity, and the tendency of consumption and investment to fall below levels that would ensure full employment, creates an important role for government in PK theory. This can come in the traditional form of government spending on public goods and services, such as roads and schools, but it can also be achieved through fiscal (spending and tax) and monetary (influencing the money supply by the central bank) policy that can influence both the amount and the type of household consumption. An example of fiscal policy that would fulfill this role might be rebates for consumers who purchase electric cars or increase the energy efficiency of their homes. Generally, PK scholars argue that fiscal policy should be driven by the need to ensure sufficient demand to create full employment as opposed to more conventional concerns about the need to balance government budgets. Monetary policy should also be driven by the need to expand demand. This is most obviously achieved through following a low interest-rate policy that promotes borrowing to increase household consumption and firm investment (Tymoigne and Wray, 2013; Lavoie, 2019).

An important current example of PK-style policy is the Green New Deal (GND) that has been proposed by some Democrats in the US Congress. The GND proposes spending whatever is necessary to green the economy (for example, by generating electricity from renewable and zero-emissions power), ensuring high-wages and full-employment, and equalizing economic opportunity by providing services such as free access to public colleges (Ocasio-Cortez, 2019). The GND is an incredibly wide-ranging proposal that would dramatically reshape economic priorities in the US, which reflects a number of PK tenets. First, government must take an active role in directing the economy toward desirable social ends, because the private sector, left to its own devices, will not always do so. In the GND, this is illustrated by the need to use active policy to shift away from environmentally destructive consumption and investment patterns. Second, government has an obligation to pursue a policy of full employment. Third, the ability of a sovereign nation to borrow, tax and create money means that even these ambitious policies are well within the financial reach of government (Nersisyan and Wray, 2019). As we will see in chapter 5, the PK GND emphasis on growth in employment conflicts in some important ways with how others would solve environmental problems. So, in the PK view, low demand is a problem sufficiently serious that it ought not to be left up to markets to solve. States can and should manage demand levels (of which consumption is a crucial part) – mostly to keep them high enough to ensure full employment.

The Evolution of Capitalist Commodity Consumption in the US after World War II

While there are elements of the relationship between firms and customers, such as the need for companies to realize profits, which are universal in capitalism, there are others that vary with the changing economic context in which firms operate and the manner in which their profits are made. Two closely related theories – social structure of accumulation (Bowles et al., 1986; Kotz, 2015) and the regulation school (Aglietta, 1979) – help provide an interpretation of the evolution of consumption in the United States after World War II through a political economy lens.

The forty post-war years are sometimes referred to as the period of "monopoly capitalism." This refers to an increase in the concentration of ownership of firms compared to earlier periods. In part, this was driven by changes that were instigated by successful demands to end the dangerous *laissez-faire* approach to consumer regulation in the early decades of the 1900s outlined in chapter 1. For example, when rules regulating food production and purity were brought in, they disadvantaged small producers and encouraged a move from natural to industrial techniques. Concentration was also driven by the introduction of principles of specialization and its accompanying increase in machinery, especially that of the assembly line, which meant that larger firms had a cost advantage over smaller firms in many industries.

With wistful hindsight, the period of monopoly capitalism is also sometimes called "the golden age" of US capitalism. It marked a period in which workers achieved more success than in any other period (before or since) in transforming the broad environment surrounding the labour market in their favour – governments were following full-employment macro-economic policy, union recognition was legally mandated (employers had to collectively bargain with unions), minimum wages were increased, and unemployment insurance was introduced. The result was relatively stable employment and increasing wages for workers – even for those at the bottom of the income distribution (Kotz, 2015). Growing wages had two crucial effects. First, they created a further incentive for firms to bring in labour-saving technology, most obviously the assembly line, which in turn increased productivity, allowed for more wage increases, and opened the door for yet more labour militancy because of the ease with which workers could shut down production (Fine, 2002: 94). Second, they resulted in income gains for a much broader section of society than had been the case in the past, particularly for "blue collar" workers, who could now afford to own homes, cars and the much desired white picket fence stereotyped as part of the ideal suburban lifestyle. A famous example of this was the Ford automobile company, which pioneered standardized assembly-line production techniques (Henry Ford once famously quipped: "Any customer can have a car painted any color that he wants so long as it is black") and made a dramatic decision to pay its workers $5 a day – twice that paid by other companies. The connection between assembly-line productivity, high wages and broad-based consumer demand characterized by Ford became so widespread that another name for this period is Fordism (Aglietta, 1979).

A crucial feature of the monopoly phase of capitalism was the large gap between production costs and selling price (Dawson, 2003). While this gap suggests success in creating surplus value, the problem in monopoly capitalism was the realization of this potential profitability without reducing prices (Baran and Sweezy, 1966). Large corporations engaged in a wide variety of techniques to increase sales, including marketing, improving existing products and discovering new ones.

The desire of individual firms to create a brand identity to separate their products from those of the rest of their competitors is a longstanding practice. If people view products as identical and interchangeable, they will simply buy the cheapest one on offer, creating price competition between sellers and reducing profits. If people have a preference for one brand over another (termed product differentiation), firms can charge a higher price, and brand-loyal customers will still purchase the product. Rather than having people buy something that they think of as "bananas," with no distinction between different companies, an ad in Germany entreated fruit lovers to "Forget the word 'banana'! Remember Chiquita!" (Haug, 1986: 26). In industries with fewer competitors, it is easier for firms to avoid price competition and compete on the basis of their brand, which, as the term "monopoly capitalism" suggests, became increasingly the case during the post-war decades. Rather than automobile companies competing by offering something called a "car" at the lowest possible price, they attracted consumers by differentiating a Ford from a Buick, frequently through the style and amenities in the vehicle.

These factors combined to create a period that featured standardized, relatively cheap mass-produced items sold to a wide section of the working class. Cultural products and services followed the same logic. Perhaps the most famous example in services is McDonald's, which rose to become a staple of American dining by offering assembly-line produced, identical meals in every location (Haug, 1986: 22–3; Harvey, 1990: 135; Bonneuil and Fressoz, 2015: 164). Consumption during monopoly capitalism was conditioned by the broad-based income gains as a result of changes in the labour market, changes in production practices, and the manner in which firms competed with one another.

The crucial caveat to this story is that mass consumption extended unevenly across social groups, and not everyone shared in the bounty. Crucial supports to mass consumption in the form of credit, mortgage guarantees and tax advantages were unequally distributed along class, race and gender lines. As Cohen points out, in the unprecedented home-ownership boom of the post-war period, "men benefited over women, whites over blacks, and middle-class Americans over working-class ones" (Cohen, 2004: 237). This helped entrench existing economic inequalities and social divisions substantially, with effects felt to this day. We look in greater detail at consumption's connections with class and with gender in chapter 6, but race has also been a huge determinant of whether and under what terms people were admitted to the consumer society. African Americans were systematically excluded from home-ownership in specific neighbourhoods through the banks' process of "redlining" and other tactics developed by white home-owners and realtors. The legacy of this is that, while the white home-ownership rate in the US is about 73 percent, the rate for Latinx Americans is 46 percent and that for African Americans 43 percent (Perry, 2019). Racially segregated access to retail and entertainment spaces persisted in law until the passage of the hard-won Civil Rights Act in 1964, and racial discrimination in credit markets and retail spaces endures in various naked and subtle forms today (Pittman, 2017; Stillerman, 2015: 102–3).

Nonetheless, the post-war period saw, on aggregate, an enormous expansion of consumption as part of the monopoly capitalist system that started to stagger in the

1970s. Some political economists trace the downfall of monopoly capitalism to factors that jeopardized the manner in which firms were making profits. Profitability in monopoly capitalism was based on improvements in technology that allowed for mass production and widespread income growth that permitted mass consumption. It worked as long as productivity increased, so that wages could continue to grow without cutting into profits, and as long as wage increases were spent on what firms were producing. Unfortunately, both of these criteria stopped being met, at least in the US. Increasing international competition through the 1960s and 1970s meant that American firms had more trouble selling their products even as household consumption continued to grow. Productivity also slowed, but a relatively heavily unionized workforce, especially in manufacturing, was still getting wage increases. To make matters worse as far as firms were concerned, the government was increasing the costs to firms through growing regulation (the Environmental Protection Agency and the Occupational Safety and Health Administration, for example, were introduced in 1970) (Harvey, 1990: 9; Kotz, 2015).

The post-1980 political economy that emerged in the US has been termed "flexible accumulation" – involving flexible labour, flexible capital and flexible patterns of consumption (Harvey, 1990: 9) – "post-Fordist" (Jessop, 1997) or, perhaps more popularly, "neoliberal" (Kotz, 2015). Flexible labour referred to business becoming more hostile to what it considered to be its overly protected, and therefore inflexible and overpaid, employees, abandoning their previous commitments to long-term employment and collective bargaining. Production was shifted to lower wage nations. Unions were fought with increasing intensity (Bronfenbrenner, 2009; Ehrenreich, 2016). In realizing these goals, the business community sought wide-ranging changes to labour market policies. The real minimum wage fell, social assistance rates dropped and their duration became more limited, the legal environment made it more difficult to form and maintain unions, and between the late 1970s and the late 1990s high interest rate monetary policy increased unemployment. The changes in the labour market reflected broader changes in the period of flexible accumulation that sought to eliminate rules that constrained the profits of firms. Services such as education were transferred from government to private-sector delivery. Regulation, such as workplace safety or financial industry oversight, was weakened and less vigorously enforced. Free trade and free movement of finance was enshrined in international agreements such as the World Trade Organization (Kotz, 2015).

These changes had important impacts on consumption in terms of both incomes and types of production. In contrast to monopoly capitalism's broad-based income gains, flexible accumulation offered disproportionate gains to those with higher incomes and very little to almost everyone else. Between 1973 and 2000 the average real income of the bottom 90 percent of US taxpayers fell by 7 percent. Incomes of the top 1 percent rose by 148 percent, the top 0.1 percent by 343 percent, and the top 0.01 percent by an amazing 599 percent (Piketty and Saez, 2003). To put it another way, in 1965, the average pay of the CEOs at the top 350 US firms (ranked by sales) stood at about twenty times the average compensation of their workers. By 2011, it was over 200 times (Mishel, 2012).

The policies enacted during the period of flexible accumulation also contributed to increases in debt. This was, in part, due to changes in the financial industry facilitated by deregulation. Regulations on the criteria that borrowers needed to meet in order to receive a loan were reduced, as were rules restricting the kinds of institutions that could offer loans and the types of loans that could be offered. For example, the down payment required for housing loans dropped from 20 percent to, in some cases, nothing (Wiedenhoft-Murphy, 2016). One example of where these practices were particularly problematic was the expansion of the subprime mortgage market (loans made to borrowers with higher risk of default), which helped fuel the bubble in the US housing market between the late 1990s and the crash of 2008 (Kotz, 2015). Debt also increased because of overarching policy changes during this period. For example, reductions in government support for post-secondary education meant that tuition increased dramatically, greatly increasing student loans (Cahalan and Perna, 2015). With workers facing stagnant or falling real wages, borrowing to finance consumption also became an increasingly necessary option (Manning, 2000; Kotz, 2015). Companies found that extending credit was a lucrative addition to their usual business of actually producing goods and services. In the mid-1980s, the ratio of total debt to personal disposable income in the US stood at about 60 percent of income. By 2007, it topped out at 138 percent, before falling slightly to 128 percent in 2009 after the economic crash (Allegretto, 2011: 21). As a result, a larger portion of household income was handed over to the financial sector through the increasingly habitual interest (including mortgage) payments of households (Pietrykowski, 2009: 6–8; Baragar and Chernomas, 2012). It is worth noting that there is nothing inevitable or universal about this situation. Other nations, such as Japan, with different attitudes toward saving and lower income inequality, had much lower personal debt levels (Stillerman, 2015).

The manner in which the credit market disadvantaged or excluded people was also different than in monopoly capitalism. Rather than refusing minorities or those on low incomes access to credit, as was previously the case, many different types of financial institutions were eager to loan to these groups, but on terms that would have at one time been described as usurious. For example, subprime mortgages were extended to many who would have previously been rejected as bad credit risks. In order to ensure that profits could be made off borrowers more likely to default, lenders charged higher interest rates. The difference between a subprime and a regular interest rate could result in borrowers paying an additional $70,000 over the life of a $100,000 loan (Wherry et al., 2019). Those on low incomes with poor credit scores are often forced into short-term, unsecured loans called payday loans or cash advances, where annual interest rates averaged 391 percent. Unsurprisingly, low-income borrowers find these loans difficult to pay off, requiring them to re-borrow in a cycle of extended indebtedness (Bennett, 2019). The tremendous expansion of credit-card use during this period is also more expensive for those on lower incomes. Those who pay off their card every month essentially receive interest-free loans, while those forced to roll over their credit-card debt incur substantial interest payments.

The freedom of lenders to set such high interest rates reflects the withdrawal of regulatory oversight during this period, favouring lending firms over borrowing households. The government could set limits on interest rates, and has done so in the past. For example, the 2006 Military Lending Act places a cap on annual interest rates at 36 percent for active-duty service members (Kantwill and Peterson, 2019). This could be extended to the entire population, which would dramatically alter the context in which lenders and borrowers interact.

The changes in credit during this period have to be placed in the context of the conflict between buyers and sellers that we have argued is common to commodity production. Lenders' profits are increased by higher interest rates and greater debt (as long as it is repaid), neither of which is advantageous to the borrower. The expansion of credit-card use was in part the result of a massive marketing effort featuring mail-outs of "pre-approved" cards and ads with celebrities pitching the freedom of instant cash ("Have it the way you want it with Visa") (Manning, 2000). Of course, credit-card companies (and payday lenders) would much prefer that people not pay off their balance every month and refer to diligent repayers as "deadbeats" (Wiedenhoft-Murphy, 2016). Because subprime interest rates were higher than those for regular mortgages, lenders would frequently sign borrowers up for subprime loans even when they qualified as regular borrowers. Lenders also enticed people with a variety of tempting but dangerous types of loans. For example, an interest-only loan allows borrowers to pay just the interest on the loan for the first years, but payments balloon in later years because repayment of the principle is compressed in the back end of the loan (Hudson, 2009: 56). The point of these examples is not that credit is bad or that it inevitably disadvantages the debtor but that the extent to which credit will be beneficial to borrowers depends on the powers they bring to the inter-action compared to lenders and the legislative environment regulating the credit industry.

In flexible accumulation, increasing consumption was very different from that which occurred in monopoly capitalism because it was accompanied by an unsustainable build-up of household debt. This was the cause of the economic collapse of 2008 that resulted in unemployment rates spiking to 10 percent and many people losing their homes in mortgage defaults. An analysis of consumption without an analysis of the broader context in which it occurs, from the deregulation of finance to changes in the labour market, would be incomplete.

The second change in consumption caused by flexible accumulation was the manner in which products were provided. The movement of manufacturing away from wealthy nations increased the distance between production and consumption. Chapter 1 explained that long-distance trade is nothing new and that geographic expansion has always been a fundamental dynamic in capitalism as firms look for new markets for their products, new sources of raw materials, and lower cost production locations. However, compared to the period of monopoly capitalism, advances in transportation and communication technology, as well as deliberate policy changes such as free trade agreements, created an expansion of global trade. This was particularly true of goods and services that do not have an actual physical form, such as electronic content from music, to apps, to call centers, where production can take place anywhere and consumables can be delivered instantly and at no cost.

The increasingly globalized sites of production, along with more flexible working conditions and the stagnation of incomes for many US earners, created the ideal conditions for the rise of discount shopping. Discount stores have a long history, from the old-timey "5 and dime" stores to Kmart's rise in the late 1900s. The growth of discount shopping and the issues that surround it were epitomized by Walmart's rise to become the largest private employer in the US, with 1.5 million employees in 2015 (Walmart, 2020). Walmart has been praised for its democratizing role of making consumption available to those with limited incomes. On the other hand, it has been criticized for paying its workers poverty-level wages and benefits, using its market power to force down the prices paid to its suppliers to unsustainably unprofitable levels, and purchasing stock from low-cost global suppliers with predictably poor labour and environmental records (Fishman, 2006).

We have argued that premature (at least as far as the customer is concerned) obsolescence is an inevitable tactic of a firm looking to realize profits. The period of flexible accumulation featured an acceleration and expansion of this process, especially as it applied to stylistic obsolescence. The acceleration refers to the turnaround time of the fashion cycle, so things were deemed "out" much more quickly than was the case even in monopoly capitalism. The expansion is the application of the idea of trends that was pioneered most obviously in clothing into a much wider variety of products and even activities, such as leisure and sports. If snowboarding is yesterday's sport, then it's time to buy a new set of skis. According to Harvey, this further reinforces the virtues of instant gratification and disposability (Harvey, 1990: 285–7). We will take up the debate about other implications of this trend in chapter 4, but, for this section, it will suffice to note that these trends should not be considered as inevitable, or even as the result of changing consumer preferences, but the most recent incarnation of firms' attempts to decrease the lifespan of products.

Some analysts have argued that this was also the period in which the consumer society became both broader and deeper (Klein, 2000). It became broader in the sense that more goods and services were purchased through the market and the promotion of those goods and services took up more physical space than in the past. People purchased more "ready to eat" meals rather than preparing food in the home, and even domestic chores were subject to Martha Stewart's commodification of the joys of home baking. Production was shifted from the public sector to the private sector, bringing more consumption under the logic of the commodity. People came into contact with more product promotions, in more places. To take professional sports as one example, Pittsburgh's football team used to play at Three Rivers Stadium, named after the three rivers that run through the city. They now play at Heinz Field, named after a ketchup brand.

Online shopping takes this broadening a big step forward. One aspect of online shopping is that it is always there, at every moment and in every place. We never leave the digital marketplace, or, more accurately, it never leaves us. As Jonathan Crary notes in his critique of the "24/7" nature of contemporary existence, "there are now very few significant interludes of human existence ... that have not been penetrated and taken over as work time, consumption time, or marketing time" (Crary, 2013: 15). Our immersive engagement with digital devices means that we are potentially always either at the office or the mall, and, as our lives are increasingly both mediated and disrupted by these devices and the networks to which they provide access, that potential is increasingly realized. As we work, relax, learn, communicate and build a shared culture through online platforms, there are fewer and fewer moments of respite from the market and from its relentless efforts to recruit us into consumption. Those who stress continuity would no doubt claim that this is less a transformation and more a continuous evolution, and it is true that people have been decrying the spread of marketing and market-based purchasing since the practices began, but their dramatic expansion marks an important change in degree from one period to another.

The deepening of post-1980 consumption refers to the belief that people's market consumption forms an increasingly important role in the formation of a personal identity, which is why it is sometimes termed "lifestyle consumption." Driven by income gains for the rich, part of this was the transformation from mass-produced goods for the home, such as a vacuum, to services that confer status, such as a country club membership or dream vacation (Berg, 2012: 173). However, according to Naomi Klein, more was going on. During the post-war decades, advertising had been shifting slowly from touting the physical properties of products to creating a more emotional association. Rather than focusing on the fuel efficiency of a car, advertisers more aggressively fetishized it, concentrating on its ability to provide the owner with power and freedom (Zukin, 2005; Stillerman, 2015). Klein argued that cutting-edge companies in the 1990s continued on this path. In fact, firms were no longer even selling products. They were merely selling their brand. The product became merely a vehicle for the brand's promotion (Klein, 2000). Nike doesn't really produce shoes. It produces the lifestyle associations of fitness, competitiveness and success. In using particular purchases to express who they are and what they stand for, people develop a strong emotional attachment to the brand. While Klein identified an important new trend, it was driven by the underlying logic of expanding sales for a profit-maximizing firm and should be placed in the context of the more longstanding practice of attempting to create strong brand identification and loyalty.

The identity emphasis of branding tapped very successfully into the growing rejection of standardization and the rise of the counterculture that started in the 1960s (Zukin, 2005). People increasingly used (and sometimes subverted) the lifestyles conveyed by those brands to forge and display their own identity. As we highlighted with the Coachella example in chapter 1, in this sense consumption has a productive aspect. Rather than just a bunch of stuff in your house, your purchases make a statement about who you are and what you value. Looking at the example of influencers in the introduction, it is clear that their commodity-filled lifestyles also act as an advertising platform to induce others to consume.

Finally, the use of marketing to elicit consumption, which, as we saw in chapter 1, has been around for ages, has been refined and developed by firms into a much more effective tool for manipulating potential customers. In the early 1900s, Frederick Taylor used time and motion studies to radically transform the workplace from one in which workers had considerable discretion over their jobs to one where their tasks and even their movements were dictated to them by management in order to increase workplace efficiency. Similarly, the realm of consumption has been transformed by the "Taylorian engineering of the objects and environments that condition ordinary people's product-related activities" (Dawson, 2003: 34). Dawson distinguished between the "sales approach" typical of monopoly capitalism of the 1950s, in which the goal of sales departments was to sell the products that were being produced, and the current "marketing approach," in which sales departments control all other corporate functions. Every step in the production process, from innovation, to design, to packaging, is dictated by the corporation's intimate knowledge of what will induce people to buy their products. In doing this, companies have developed increasingly sophisticated tools to track, understand and manipulate their potential customers. Firms analyze credit- and debit-card purchases, email messages and loyalty reward programs. They do in-depth interviewing in careful focus groups, all to gain a greater understanding of consumers in order to refine and target their messaging in a manner that will more efficiently induce sales (Stillerman, 2015).

Shoshana Zuboff (2019) shows how the corporate giants of the digital economy such as Google and Facebook profit from such tracking and influencing of our online behaviour: 84 percent of Google's $161.8 billion in revenue in 2019 was from advertising (Alphabet, 2019: 24). Our consumption practices, along with allegedly non-commercial activities such as searching, chatting, posting or "liking," are micro-surveilled and logged to predict our future behaviour and, more menacingly, to influence it so that it conforms to the prediction. This leaps from the online into the real world through behavioural data-collection devices such as FitBits, "smart" thermostats and household digital "assistants" (Amazon's Alexa or Google Home). Through all of these, we provide to corporations incredibly detailed information about our lives which is, in turn, processed into predictive models and further adapted into mechanisms for manipulating our behaviour (Zuboff, 2019: 25; Pridmore and Lyon, 2011).

As was the case with monopoly capitalism, the evolution of consumption in the US (whether that is the growth in household debt, the rise of Walmart or the growth of Google tracking) is subject to the overarching dynamics of capitalist commodity production and historically specific conditions of profitability in different time periods and different regions.

Conclusion

The theory put forward in this chapter places consumption in the context of the political economic system – capitalism – in which it occurs. The hallmark of this system is that firms create the potential for profit in their production process and realize that potential through the sale of their products. This can create conflict with households, whose members are both an important cost to be minimized in production and a revenue source to be maximized in consumption. The extent to which households will achieve their goal of the "sustenance and enjoyment of life" will depend both on the power wielded in decisions by individual firms and people in the market and their collective efforts to alter the larger policy environment in which those decisions occur. Households are both the final arbiters of what firms can sell and, in a democracy, the policies that government implements. Firms must use slightly more subtle arts of persuasion on the consumer and in the political system, which they have come to wield with increasing sophistication. Companies have been relatively successful in maintaining a policy environment favourable to their ability to influence people.

Using their individual right of refusal, people do ensure that products for which they have no use are not churned out by firms, at least not over the long term. Households can alter, and have altered, the manner in which firms communicate to them, increasing information and accuracy. Households can remove, and have removed, some things from the realm of commodity production when that system proved detrimental to people's well-being. However, these tend to be the exceptions rather than the everyday rule. Generally speaking, over time, more things are brought into the realm of commodity production than are removed. Corporations devise more methods to target and influence people than are restricted. Understanding consumption requires an understanding of the economic system and the powers that households and corporations wield in that system generally, as well as of how those change in different regions and different historical periods.

4

Private Choices, Social Problems

Introduction

Let's return to the shops. The manner in which the shirt was purchased in chapter 2 left the consumer, no doubt, feeling quite pleased with herself. She was now in possession of a fine garment, in which she could confidently stride into tomorrow's big meeting. Most likely, she also felt a little frisson of excitement for finding just the right thing that she had been looking for. This feel-good story follows straightforwardly from the analysis of consumption presented in chapter 2, and there is a degree of accuracy to it. If the consumer had tried on an ill-fitting shirt with wretched colouring, chances are poor they would have bought it.

Yet it is also an incomplete truth that disguises a great deal about the purchasing decision. Crucially, it ignores both human frailties and social context. On the frailty side, people often make repeated, predictable consumption decisions that actually make them worse off. We are also social animals. Our wardrobe is influenced by the society around us – those whose opinions we value (including those we will never meet, as every good Instagram influencer knows) and the firms that need us to buy. What seemed like a sensible bit of cloth a decade ago now looks like the height of absurdity. Far from being a monument to good decisions, many closets are a graveyard of disuse and regret. This chapter will analyze, and place in a political economy context, theories that attempt to explain why consumption might not actually benefit the consumer.

What You Don't Know Might Hurt You: Information Asymmetry

Most people spend considerably more time researching the purchase of a car than that of a new shirt. Yet, despite people's careful reading of consumer reports and extensive searching through Google reviews, the market for used cars is a notorious example of the problems of consumer information in a free and voluntary market exchange. The seller of a used car likely knows more about its past history than the buyer (termed information asymmetry between buyer and seller) – whether it has been driven hard with Tokyo drift-style braking or at a more sedate pace that would encourage longevity (Akerlof, 1970).

The problem of information asymmetry comes in varying degrees of perniciousness. The used car is an "experience good" (Akerlof, 1970) in which the quality of the product is unknown before its purchase but is revealed in its use. At least with experience goods, consumers will eventually have some idea of whether they have been ripped off (Nelson, 1970). A more intractable problem is presented by the "credence good," whose quality fails to reveal itself even in its use. Even within the broad category of credence goods there are different levels of intractability. One version occurs when consumers do not know the kind of good or service that they need but can observe the consequences of what they get, albeit in a fairly indirect way.

A common example of this would be a trip to the auto mechanic. When people take their car in, they know that something is wrong, but they most likely don't know precisely what repairs need to be made. When they get the car back from the shop, they can often tell whether their car is running better, but they most likely won't know if the services at the garage were the appropriate and necessary ones (Darby and Karni, 1973). In an even more problematic category of credence goods, quality is impossible to determine by using the product. Examples of this are labelling or certification schemes such as organic or Fairtrade (a topic to which we will return in chapter 7). No amount of tasting is going to reveal whether your lettuce is produced according to the standards promised by the organic label. In this case, the high degree of information asymmetry can open the door for abuses by firms that promise the consumer one thing but deliver something substantially inferior.

Information asymmetry creates a problem for both the assumption of the well-informed consumer and the comforting conclusions about the benefits of consumption that can flow from it. If consumers do not fully understand the utility they receive from their purchases, their ability to choose between products to maximize their utility is also compromised. There are crucially important categories of goods that fall under this umbrella beyond car repairs and organic spinach. Returning to the example of health-care consumption from chapter 2, doctors, or other suppliers of health services, have better information than their patients on what treatments will be necessary and effective. A famous study by the Rand Corporation in the 1970s found that, when asked to pay for treatments, patients dropped those that were incredibly beneficial as well as those of more dubious benefit, showing that people have difficulty evaluating the benefits of different kinds of medical care (Newhouse, 1993: 339). As a result of people's understandable lack of knowledge, their demand for health services is more a matter of doctor's orders than it is consumer preferences. As is the case with a mechanic, this creates considerable scope for overtreatment. Studies have shown that, when doctors own medical facilities (for example, labs) or technology, such as magnetic resonance imaging (MRI) machines, they prescribe their own services more often than doctors who do not have an ownership stake (Bernstein, 2009). Another study found that the rate of surgery was 78 percent higher when doctors were paid per treatment compared to capitation (fee per patient), despite similar patient characteristics (Shafrin, 2010; see also Hemenway et al., 1990; Hillman et al., 1989).

Clearly, not all goods or services suffer from information asymmetry and, even for those that do, the problems may not be as damaging as they first appear. In the absence of complete information, brands, and the advertising that backs them, may act as a signal of quality to consumers. The expense of advertising is only worthwhile if it can be recouped through expanded and repeat sales. A firm producing a sub-par product is less likely to spend money on an ad campaign because, once its poor quality became known (in the case of an experience good) or exposed (in the case of a credence good), its expenditure will not generate additional sales. The mere fact that firms are willing to spend money on ads means that they must be providing goods of high quality (Nelson, 1974). Department stores may play a similar role. If the items on their shelves, and the advertising spent promoting them, are going to pay off they need repeat customers, which is only possible if they stock goods of high quality. In this interpretation, department stores act to vet the quality of the merchandise they hold, saving consumers the time-consuming process of doing their own research on the brands (Stigler, 1961). The idea of signalling not only rescues the idea that consumers get what they want from their consumption dollar; it simultaneously provides a positive *raison d'être* for advertising, no matter how information-free its content.

The discussion so far presents information asymmetry as something inherent in the characteristics of the good, like a used car or an ethical label. However, chapter 3 suggests that information is an arena of conflicting interests between firms and consumers. Consumers would like accurate information with which to judge products, while firms are interested in providing information that will increase sales. The two can often conflict. To just take one example, there has been an ongoing battle between the US food industry and its customers over both the scientific evidence on the health impacts of different foods and how that information is presented. The World Health Organization recommended daily adult intake of sugar is six teaspoons. US adults gobble up twenty-two (Friedman, 2014). The sugar industry funds research that deliberately seeks to downplay the link between weight gain and sugar in an effort to cloud consumers' understanding of the impact of sugar consumption (Bes-Rastrollo et al., 2013). It has also lobbied the Food and Drug Administration (FDA) for favourable wording in US food and dietary guidelines (Nestle, 2013) and is attempting to give less information on packaging. The industry wants the amount of sugar presented in grams, a unit that means very little to American consumers, who don't really know if 50 grams is a lot of sugar. When the US government attempted to bring in different guidelines that would make the amount more understandable (by introducing how much of the recommended daily value of sugar was in the container) the industry fought vigorously against the change. Similar battles are fought over whether genetically modified products should have a GMO label and virtually every other information regulation that would harm firms' sales.

Conclusions about the extent of the difficulty posed by information asymmetry create very different policy recommendations. If brands and advertising provide quality, then the conclusions from chapter 2 about the usefulness of the market as an efficient provider of what the consumer wants and needs still hold. If, on the other hand, sellers in a wide variety of contexts can use consumer ignorance to swindle them in more or less egregious ways, then it opens the door for a wide variety of government interventions that attempt to crack down on such abuses. It was concerns about the inability of patients to judge the effectiveness of drugs that spawned the drug testing requirements at the FDA. Health inspections were designed to compensate for the fact that diners do not know the extent of hand-washing in their favourite restaurant.

You're Not as Clever as You Think: Behavioural Economics

Even if consumers had access to full information, the behavioural economics of George Katona discussed in chapter 2 raise another problem. Subsequent behaviouralists incorporated research from other disciplines, most obviously psychology, to argue that people do not behave, and are not cognitively capable of behaving, in the optimizing manner outlined in chapter 2 (Lavoie, 1994: 545). Rather, they have "bounded rationality," which means that, because there are limits on people's knowledge and ability to process information, they rely on a wide variety of short-hand tendencies or rules of thumb to make decisions, which often produce choices that are less than optimal (Simon, 1982; Kahneman, 2003; Schwartz, 2004; Thaler, 2008).

We will focus on a couple of examples that are particularly germane to consumption decisions. First, people's choices can be influenced by how they are framed. For example, people will make different choices depending on how those choices are presented (Kahneman and Tversky, 1979; Tversky and Kahneman, 1981). This research shows that consumers can be fairly easily manipulated by firms into spending more. To take one example, if a computer seller offers a package with a large number of features and gives customers the option to pare down their purchase, people are likely to spend more than if the seller offers a more basic model and gives customers the option of adding to their purchase (Biswas, 2009). Another common example is that, because people often evaluate prices in relation to other prices they see, firms can manipulate purchasing. In restaurants, few individuals want the stigma that goes with ordering the cheapest wine, so the wine with the largest mark-up is usually the second cheapest. Generally, firms are well aware of how to manipulate their customers through these framing devices (Samson, 2014).

A second example is the idea of time bias – that people irrationally value their current selves more than their future selves. They will do too many things that they currently like that will cause pain in the future and not do enough things that are painful in the present but would benefit them in the future. As a result, people don't make decisions that maximize their utility over time. For example, they have a choice between spending, which creates the pleasure of current consumption, and saving, which delays that pleasure into the future. Because forgoing current consumption is painful, people will put it off indefinitely so that their future consumption will be less than their future selves would like (Frederick et al., 2002). In addition, many consumption items contain current pleasures but future pains, or vice versa. A delicious donut now may mean poorer health later. A painful trip to the gym now may mean less chance of heart disease later. The time bias problem suggests that individuals will eat too many donuts and make too few trips to the gym to maximize their well-being over time (O'Donoghue and Rabin, 1999).

The theory of time inconsistency and behavioural insights more generally yield very different normative conclusions than rational maximization, even when examining the same actions. If people pack on a few pounds as a result of avoiding the gym, time-consistent rational maximizing would interpret this as the sweaty costs of working out outweighing the flab-decreasing benefits and is, therefore, what the consumer wants over their lifespan. According to time inconsistency, this same action would be caused by a welfare-decreasing self-control problem. Similar conclusions can be arrived at for any behaviour in which present costs yield future benefits (or present benefits cause future costs) – from stopping smoking to looking for a job. The implication of the time-inconsistency problem is that not all individual choices can be assumed to be welfare improving.

As was the case with information asymmetry, in a political economy system driven by the need for firms to realize profits, companies are actually obligated to exacerbate behavioural frailties at the expense of consumers. Most stores place a wide variety of tasty but unhealthy treats very close to the check-out aisle, where shoppers and their children can take a good long look while stuck in line. Given people's pleasure-seeking weaknesses, a grocery store would be giving up considerable revenue by not offering these items, making it less competitive compared to its rivals that continued to pander to people's dietary weaknesses (Akerlof and Shiller, 2015). This is a very different conclusion than the one adopted in chapter 2 by Friedman, who argued that a competitive market would minimize bad firm behaviour.

Relative Consumption

It might also be possible that what we want is heavily dependent on what everyone else has. Conceptualizing consumption as an individual decision, made to satisfy individual desires, artificially abstracts from the fact that individual decisions are conditioned by society at large. An early recognition of this came from Adam Smith. Writing in 1776, he argued that individual consumption is conditioned by the "customary" level established by broader society.

Smith pointed out that necessities went beyond what is needed for mere survival. Rather, necessities are "whatever the custom of the country renders it indecent for creditable people, even of the lowest order, to be without" (Smith, 1981: Book 5, chap. 2, art. 4). As an example, he argued that, while shoes were not, strictly speaking, a necessity, and many in France went barefoot without any social stigma, in England even those on the lowest rung of the social ladder would be ashamed to wander the streets without them.

There is no shortage of contemporary examples of how gender, sexuality, age, race, ethnicity, religion and class intersect to pattern our consumption. Wardrobes, grooming, ownership of electronics and furnishings, modes of transportation, even diet are all either dictated or conditioned by these social factors. Flouting these (failing to provide a diamond on an engagement) can prove socially quite costly. To take a small example, parents in a certain income bracket now feel considerable pressure to put on lavish birthday parties for their children – often hooked to a Disney film or other merchandising vehicle.

These social influences on consumption point to some important limits to the conception of individual choice presented in chapter 2. If consumption were an individual decision, people's choices would be much more randomly distributed across socio-economic groups than they are, but consumption patterns are influenced by gender, income, race and other socio-economic factors. Women, for example, purchase more clothing than men. This is not simply a matter of individual preference but reflects gender norms and expectations (Fine, 2002: 171). Essentially, consumption is as much about social and group patterns of acceptability as it is about individual preferences.

Smith's idea of relative consumption gained empirical support from economist Richard Easterlin. Using survey data in the US about people's self-reported happiness, Easterlin found that, at any moment in time, people with higher incomes were more likely to be happy than those with lower incomes, but society as a whole was no happier when overall income increased over time. Between the 1940s and the 1970s, real per capita income increased dramatically in the US, yet people did not consider themselves any happier

(Easterlin, 1974; Scitovsky, 1992: 135–6; Easterlin, 1995: 38). If we look cross-nationally, although it is clearly the case that people in France express greater life satisfaction than people in India, who in turn have greater satisfaction than people in lower income nations (Deaton, 2008), beyond a fairly low level of GDP per capita (estimates locate this around US$15,000; Jackson, 2009), even very large increases in income don't translate into increases in happiness. These findings are problematic for the view of consumption put forward in chapter 2, which implies, broadly speaking, that rising incomes will permit rising consumption and, therefore, greater satisfaction.

Easterlin's findings can be easily reconciled with a hypothesis of relative consumption, in which satisfaction from consumption depends on how an individual's consumption compares to that of others. This implies that a person with greater consumption relative to others will have greater life satisfaction. However, greater satisfaction does not necessarily derive from general increases in income and consumption (Clark et al., 2008). The general idea is that, as social creatures, we do not derive satisfaction from our consumption based merely on our intrinsic, individual preferences; rather, that the satisfaction we receive from any given level of consumption, or even individual types of consumption, depends on the expectations and preferences of those around us (see also Duesenberry, 1949; Doucouliagos, 1994; Scitovsky, 1992).

"Positional goods," which signal a mark of status or social standing in addition to reflecting a social level of customary consumption (more on this in chapter 6), can also induce consumption we might have preferred to avoid. Many of these positional goods advertise competence, which in many professions can therefore contribute to future success (Frank, 1985). For example, real-estate agents might purchase expensive cars because it signals success, making their clients believe that they move a lot of houses. A certain kind and level of outfit is often considered "appropriate for work." This sort of positional consumption (from a fancy suit on a lawyer to cosmetics on serving staff) is helpful to anyone who is trying to win over a customer, boss or colleague (ibid.). What constitutes an appropriate positional good will vary by profession, and the particulars of the specific positional item are less important than their role in creating an affinity with others. The consumption must, therefore, be a socially accepted symbol designed to illicit positive associations. Relative or positional consumption creates some important social problems. While the consumption of these products is individually rational, from a social standpoint it is "wasteful" because the satisfaction it creates for one person comes only from its relative position, which negatively impacts others and does not serve well-being as a whole. It is roughly equivalent to taking steroids in a sporting contest. While it is in each participant's individual interest to take steroids and, therefore, increase their chance of winning, the outcome is that all participants are likely to take steroids, leaving them, relatively speaking, no more likely to win than in the no-steroid contest. It would be better for the group, and indeed each individual, if no one took steroids because the battle for athletic superiority could be run at less cost for each participant. In contrast to the behaviouralists, the relativists argue that individuals may act to maximize their self-interested satisfaction, but, because of the interdependence of consumption, in doing so they actually make themselves, and society as a whole, worse off. The damage occurs as consumption shifts away from non-relative and non-positional to relative and positional and away from non-income-generating activities to income-generating activities. As an example of the former, savings is a non-positional use of income compared with spending. While a suit might be necessary to fit in at the office, putting away a couple of dollars for retirement fails to improve your relative or positional status. As an example of the latter, people will dedicate more time to earning income that fuels relative and positional consumption than in other activities, such as time relaxing with their families (Frank, 1985). According to economist Robert Frank, this kind of positional consumption is the rule rather than the exception. "The invisible hand is valid only in the special case in which each individual's rewards are completely independent of the choices made by others. In the rivalrous world we live in, precious few examples spring to mind" (Frank, 1999: 271).

For some writers, this creates a treadmill where people work harder to afford increasing levels of consumption that leave them with no more satisfaction (Schor, 1998), calling into question the very foundation of an economy based on economic growth, increasing incomes and consumption (Durning, 1992). As Frank noted, "across the board increases in the stock of material goods have no measurable impact on our psychological or physiological well-being" (Frank, 1999: 6).

Created Wants

It is also possible that what we think makes us happy and better off might be created by the firms that are meeting those wants and needs. As early as 1924, critics of consumption were arguing that, in a "modern" society, the production cart was now driving the consumption horse. "The problem before us today," they argued, "is not how to produce the goods, but how to produce the customers" (Strauss, 1924: 579). In the 1940s, Frankfurt School scholars Max Horkheimer and Theodor Adorno suggested that capitalist mass production would generate an accompanying "mass culture" – an industrially produced form of culture characterized by the consumption of homogeneous, standardized products (Adorno and Horkheimer, 1997). They were highly contemptuous of the quality of this culture and despaired of the docile consumers who were alleged to swallow it, leaving them open to a charge of cultural elitism. Nonetheless, their insights that culture might be supply-driven, and that the creation of desires becomes a significant problem as society's productive capacity rises, remain important.

When people are mired in abject poverty, their first increase in income will be spent on things that are most important – food, clothing and shelter. As those basic needs are met, further increases in income are often spent on less vital wants (Pasinetti, 1981; Schefold, 1985). However, in this context, it is not impossible that people will cease to increase their consumption and instead opt to limit their income-earning toil. For firms, this stagnation in demand would be disastrous, and so, to counter it, they must foster the desire for products that are inherently not particularly important. "Many of the desires of the individual are no longer even evident to him. They become so only as they are synthesized, elaborated and nurtured by advertising and salesmanship" (Galbraith, 1958: 2). The result, according to economist John Galbraith, is that the supply of products creates the demands of consumers. Created wants present a number of problems for the normative claim that increasing consumption will improve our well-being. Most obviously, it is no longer clear that we are actually fulfilling our own wants and needs. In addition, it skews our preferences toward things that are subject to want creation by firms. In the words of Galbraith, although an affluent society is a "well-stuffed cornucopia," people may not get what they genuinely need.

As Galbraith understood, created wants are not merely about advertising. They are also about design and trends. It is far easier to convince people successfully that their current stock of possessions and activities is inadequate if that stock is not identical to what is currently being offered in the shop window. Because coming up with genuinely new products on a sufficiently regular basis to ensure continuing high sales is no easy feat, corporations often take a second-best approach of making old products appear new by executing superficial changes to style and design (Baran and Sweezy, 1966). The fashion industry was an obvious pioneer of this tactic. As one consumption critic caustically described, for tie-sellers, a society's "tie wealth" is not a mark of a well-dressed population but a wretched impediment to current sales. The solution is not to let the tie die a natural death by unravelling but to speed its demise through sowing dissatisfaction with the existing tie stock. The commonly heard phrase "ties are getting wider" makes it sound as though ties are, of their own accord, expanding as naturally as a change in the weather, when it is in reality a change deliberately engineered by the very firms that sold you the narrower tie in the first place (Haug, 1986: 42). Firms hasten the death of many products through a variety of mechanisms in addition to trends, from deliberate design that limits durability (as was the case with the cell phone example from chapter 3) to misleading packaging that disguises the limited quantity inside (which is why there are dimples in the bottom of many containers in the grocery store) (Fine 2002; Haug, 1986: 39). As is the case with fashions trends, the purpose of these tactics is to generate demand prematurely (at least as far as the customer is concerned).

Similarly, the retail experience is designed to elicit purchases. Sales people receive training on the different "types" of customers, how to make them feel relaxed, and what interactions will make it more likely that they will have made a purchase when they walk out of the store. The presentation of commodities – the sales location, the music in the store, the look of the sales staff, and the design of the store itself – is an important component of the sales effort (Haug, 1986: 68). Indeed, the whole purpose of the retail environment is to overcome buyers' reluctance to part with their money and provoke a purchase that would not otherwise be made.

For Galbraith, advertising and marketing have two important effects, one obviously intended, the other more subtle. The first is to increase people's desire for a particular product. While not every advertisement or marketing effort is successful, the companies that spend money in this way clearly think that the costs incurred pay off in terms of increased sales or they wouldn't bother to do it. In 2018, the top 200 advertisers in the US spent $163 billion on online, radio, print and TV ads (which would be only a fraction of the total marketing budget that would also include design, packaging, displays and commercial architecture). The largest, media giant Comcast, spent $6.12 billion alone (De Luce, 2019). As profit-making entities, firms would simply not spend this kind of money unless it paid off with increased revenue. It is also beyond question that many ads are very successful in creating sales. One study estimated that companies with good marketing campaigns tripled their short-term sales (Jones, 2007). A famous "how to" marketing guide attributes the success of brands such as Starbucks, Nike, Ben and Jerry's, Marlboro and Vitaminwater to their use of "cultural innovation" strategies that associate products with profound, untapped cultural shifts (Holt and Cameron, 2010). Empirical studies on the impact of advertising on sales disagree about the precise magnitude of the impact, but they agree that it is positive (Sethuraman et al., 2011).

The second is, more generally and subtly, to alter people's choices, and even values, toward achieving satisfaction through private consumption. From this perspective, marketing can be conceived as a form of (contested) power or management, which fosters certain forms of consumption and channels those into particular directions. The shortened product lifespan associated with design and aesthetics mentioned in the previous section can be extended to the role that marketing plays in fostering modern consumers who are continuously engaged in a project of self-improvement – a project that must sow dissatisfaction with the current state of life affairs (too tubby or boring) and propose a commodity-based solution (diets and exciting adventure vacations). This not only accelerates dissatisfaction with what people already have, it also proposes a "vision of the good life as the ability to consume commercially produced, private goods and services" (Zwick and Cayla, 2011: 16). Schor attempted to provide some evidence of this effect by looking at US attitude changes between the 1970s and the 1990s. In the 1970s, when asked what "the good life" meant to them, people's responses tended to be things such as a happy marriage, children, an interesting job, and a job that contributes to the welfare of society. By the 1990s, individuals responded far more often with such answers as a vacation home, a swimming pool, a second colour TV, nice clothes, a second car, a job that pays well and, more broadly, "a lot of money" (Schor, 1998: 15–16). A study of a Bombay advertising firm suggests that similar values are promoted by marketing firms in the rapidly growing emerging market. Even a product as humble as cake mix was marketed through messages of emancipation and empowerment (albeit in the sense of being able to perform traditional female roles more efficiently), in which being modern was identified with more and better individual consumer choice (Cayla and Peñaloza, 2011).

To the extent that Schor has identified a genuine change in values, it would represent an interesting conflict with evidence found by "happiness" or "well-being" research. Although a higher relative income does increase people's positive responses to questions such as "How satisfied are you with life as a whole these days?," a host of other, non-economic and even non-consumption variables, such as the quality of their government (Helliwell and Huang, 2008) and social connections at work and at home (Helliwell and Putnam,

2004) are, if anything, more important to well-being. If, as Schor suggests, people are increasingly valuing commodity-based sources of satisfaction (there is evidence that there has been a shift from "material" sources of satisfaction such as houses toward "self-expression" (Inglehart, 2007) such as vacations, but these are both, we would argue, commodified sources), evidence from well-being research suggests that they are seeking satisfaction in the wrong place.

Worse, the pursuit of commodity-based satisfaction may actually compromise other sources of well-being. If the quality of government is important, Galbraith points out that, because public services do not benefit from the process of want creation (when is the last time you saw an ad for your local public school?), they are underappreciated and starved of funding (Galbraith, 1958). For Schor, the pursuit of commodity-based satisfaction is one of the causes in the US of spiraling debt levels alongside increased household working hours. Predictably, people are also more stressed, and time spent with family and undertaking voluntary activities has dropped (Schor, 1998: 65–85), all of which compromises what well-being research suggests is important to life satisfaction. Schor encouraged individuals to change their attitudes toward consumption by eschewing "commodified leisure," embracing their unfashionable kitchen, and ignoring the latest clothing trends. She advocated a sharing economy on a very different model than that prescribed by Airbnb or Uber by recommending clothing swaps among friends and communal lawn mowers among neighbours. Finally, people should volunteer for community organizations, especially those that are dedicated to consumer issues around reducing spending (Schor, 1998).

In encouraging people to throw off the shackles of consumerism, Schor echoes other previous thinkers, including John Stuart Mill writing in the mid-1800s. It should not be a "matter of congratulation that persons who are already richer than anyone needs to be, should have doubled their means of consuming things which give little or no pleasure except as representative of wealth." Human creativity should turn to "improving the Art of Living," which would involve cultivating more intellectual and cultural pursuits (Mill, 1885: 593–5). In *Walden*, his tribute to anti-materialism, Henry

Thoreau published his Spartan monthly spending to demonstrate how little purchasing was necessary to live what he described as a comfortable existence ($61.99, which included building a house, but as a cost-saving measure he did eat a woodchuck – "musky flavour") (Thoreau, 1854: 66). This genre of critique became increasingly popular in the 1960s, focusing on how consumerism created shallowly undesirable human traits. The merits of rejecting the superficial trappings of consumer luxury in favour of a more intellectual (or even spiritual) life of voluntary simplicity appear in many works, including those of Gandhi and E. F. Schumacher's *Small is Beautiful* (1973).

Those who argue that satisfaction cannot, or should not, be bought through consumption have been criticized from very different perspectives. On one hand, they are censured for being intellectual snobs who impose their own elitist views of "desirable" pursuits. Is time spent working to afford a nice car really inferior on the moral ladder to time spent contemplating the meaning of life? Similarly, it downplays the benefits of continued increases in consumption and production. Few in today's affluent nations would agree with Mill's claim that people in his day were "richer than anyone needed to be." Critics derisively describe the likes of Schor, Mill and Thoreau as the "hair shirt" brigade (after the scratchy clothing worn by monks who deliberately denied themselves even the most rudimentary material comfort) (Hilton, 2003: 317).

Another quite different criticism is that encouraging people to be less materialistic is unlikely to be successful in an overarching context that makes those changes incredibly difficult. Currently, firms bombard people with want-creation messages, making anti-consumerist lifestyles less likely. But, as we argued previously, this is a result of a public policy environment that could be changed. However, if people focused more on "improving the Art of Living," as Mill wanted, rather than consumption, this would represent a considerable problem for firms' ability to realize profits.

The Androcentric Consumer

Feminist economists add to critiques of consumption (and pioneered some of them) by emphasizing that, from Adam Smith onward, the operation of markets has been characterized as a manifestation of a self-regarding, asocial human nature (Nelson, 1996). In this view, to engage self-interestedly in exchange is not a learned orientation but to swim with the current of what it means to be human (Marçal, 2016). However, the feminist critique has pointed out that this is an utterly male-centric model. Women, having often been assigned roles at odds with self-interest and tasked with caring mostly for others, have frequently been socialized to seek well-being (social acceptance) not through advancing their own interests but in looking out for others.

Relatedly, the assumption that humans seek and measure their welfare independent of the welfare of others flies in the face of much of women's experience. Feminist theory suggests that individual well-being is both relative to and dependent on the well-being of others. Interpersonal comparison – forbidden in the neoclassical economics of consumption – is undeniable from a feminist perspective. Paula England suggests that the entire edifice of assumptions underlying neoclassical welfare economics is based on a male-centered idea of the "separative self," foreign to women's socialization and experience (England, 1993). It is no coincidence that a female economist – Hazel Kyrk, writing in 1923 – was among the early critics of the neoclassical utility theorists, claiming that "we cannot recognize ourselves or our fellows in the hedonistic, individualistic calculators whom they described, nor find in their account any trace of the complexity of motives, impulses and interests which lie behind market activities" (Kyrk, 2010: 178).

Feminist economists have also criticized the measure of consumption as currently practiced in national income accounts because it limits "consumption" to the sum total of final goods and services purchased in the market. This is profoundly misleading and ignores completely the necessary contributions of non-market forms of production and consumption to human well-being, quality of life and productive capacities (O'Hara, 1999). Feminist economists have insisted on integrating non-commodified forms of provisioning into the concept of consumption. Since their work is so frequently unpaid – including work that enables household consumption – a lot of women's labour "counts for nothing," as Marilyn Waring (1999) famously claimed. Much of this work, as Kyrk also pointed out early on, is related to consumption. In the standard model's neat separation of consumption and production, the many hours of work undertaken to enable consumption are made invisible. Matching household preferences with goods that might satisfy them, selecting the best of these under budget constraints, transporting them from the shops to the home, engaging in their final processing before consumption, cleaning up the by-products and waste, dealing with the emotional consequences of any failure to match goods with preferences, etc., all make for a considerable amount of work categorized as consumption.

Feminist economists point out that all of this work takes place both within and as a necessary foundation for capitalist production but also must stand apart from it in terms of its motivators, its logic and its compensation. This sphere – necessary to allow others to engage in the allegedly rational, calculating, self-regarding processes of market exchange – must be governed by a completely different (and female-assigned) set of values and orientations. Marçal (2016) uses the story of Adam Smith's mother to highlight this. Mrs Smith lived with Adam for most of his life – caring for him, bringing home the dinner self-interestedly sold to her by the butcher, brewer and baker, cooking Adam's meals, and tending to the household. Wives and mothers likely did all of this work for the butcher, the baker and the brewer as well, greasing the wheels of exchange and undertaking the work of consumption.

Conclusion

A political economy of consumption that injects a little more realism into human behaviour yields some quite different conclusions about the benefits of consumption than that presented in chapter 2. No longer are we quite as confident in the welfare-improving nature of the shirt purchase. Although information asymmetry is nothing like as terrifying a proposition when buying clothes as it is in something like choosing the right health care, you are still not completely certain about whether that shirt is going to stand up to a couple of trips through the drier. Will the colours fade or the collar fray? This information will be revealed only over time. Even worse, if you are concerned about the social conditions of the workers or the impact on the planet, it is unlikely you will ever know, although chances are overwhelming that, given current production practices, the answer will not be comforting (see chapter 7).

It is also very possible that the purchase of the shirt may actually be making you worse off. Perhaps the shirt represented a spur of the moment, impulse buy, satisfying your present-loving self's desire for a fancy bit of cloth to wear out on Friday night. Yet that Friday night swagger was placed on an already overextended credit card that your future self is going to have a very difficult time paying off. If this purchase is only one of several that racked up debt or decreased the amount that you contributed to your retirement plan, you might be creating some problems for yourself down the line.

The purchase may have been an effort to stay sartorially respectable. Perhaps, left in splendid isolation, you would have been perfectly content with your old shirt. But the shirt doesn't quite fit in when compared to the "customary" level of fashion established by broader society or to the more specific norms established by a reference group to which you belong or aspire, or of which you need the approval. In this case, the new shirt is a very reasonable purchase on an individual basis, but the collective shirt purchases to keep up with changing standards are a societal waste of resources that could have been much better spent on a non-positional good.

Finally, that new shirt's appeal might rest on the clever advertising of a well-paid marketing executive. The very shirts that last year were being touted as must-have items are second rate in comparison with this season's trends. Want creation is also important in order to place the ideas of information asymmetry, behaviouralist cognitive frailty and relative positioning in their political economy context.

The information contained in products is more or less transparent for different goods, but the desire for firms to sell products leads them either to hide the particulars available to consumers or attempt to mislead them. People may not be able to make maximizing decisions, but firms in a competitive market must prey on those foibles to maximize sales. People are social creatures, comparing their own position to that of others, but that tendency is exacerbated by the want-creation process of firms, which are continuously reminding people that their current consumption is falling behind.

In the political economy world of costs and benefits, this chapter suggests that, on both an individual and a collective basis, the benefits of consumption are not as great as they appear in the theories presented in chapter 2. In the next chapter we will turn to an important element of the cost side of the ledger.

5
The Shopocalypse?

The term "consumption," and the way that the practice of consumption is structured, hides a lot. Let's take that shirt you purchased back in chapter 2, for a start. Somewhere in the part of your brain where abstractions dwell, you know that the shirt had some history before you tried it on and found it so fetching and also that it has a future once you and it part ways. But you don't really dwell on it much. Consumption is experienced as a moment – variously long or short – at whose end an object is used up. But that shirt was up to all kinds of trouble well before you pulled it off the rack.

The trouble starts with growing cotton. While cotton takes up about 2.4 percent of the world's agricultural land, its production accounts for about 24 percent of insecticides and 11 percent of pesticides, poisoning both the land and the workers who produce it (Chapagain et al., 2006: 192; Brooks, 2015: 19). Your shirt also contains about 2,720 litres of "virtual water" (Chapagain et al., 2006: 193), most likely drawn from an area already water stressed in China, India, Pakistan or Uzbekistan. Between 1960 and 2000, the once vast Aral Sea lost 80 percent of its volume and 60 percent of its area as water from Central Asia's Amu Darya and Syr Darya – rivers that once fed the Aral Sea – was diverted for cotton irrigation.

The colours that drew your eye to this particular shirt are another source of trouble: 40 percent of the colourants used worldwide contain carcinogenic organically bound chlorine, which is present in high levels, along with non-biodegradable heavy metals, in the effluent pouring from textile mills into waterways (Khan and Malik, 2013). As the consumer, however, you are blissfully unaware of the destruction your shirt has left in its wake. In this chapter, we delve into what has recently become the most urgently discussed aspect of consumption – its environmental consequences.

By now you've very likely heard about the "Great Pacific Garbage Patch." The patch consists of an unknown but vast quantity of floating and submerged debris, composed mostly of plastics, much of which has broken down to a tiny size (dubbed "microplastics"), making the ocean waters into a kind of thin slurry, punctuated by suspended or floating chunks of garbage. It's not the only such patch in the world (just the most famous – the world's premiere celebrity garbage dump), and, indeed, plastics accumulate at varying concentrations throughout the world's oceans. They're found as distantly as in the guts of beings that inhabit the Marianas Trench – and, it turns out, as close as in our drinking water (Carrington, 2017).

The ubiquity of plastic in our environment reminds us that we rarely actually "consume" things in their entirety. They have another existence beyond our experience of them once they are transformed into waste. The OECD (2013) estimates that about 20 percent of all the material extracted in the world ends up in municipal solid waste streams.

As with your shirt, these things have a history as well as a future about which we are largely ignorant. The total percentage of waste from extraction is much higher than that captured by municipal waste streams. The same OECD paper cited above reports that, in 2008, for every ton of raw material extracted that actually went into some commodity, another 0.71 of a ton was extracted but unused. These are the by-products of extraction, such as economically non-valuable sea-life caught in the process of fishing, plant life and rock scraped or dug away in the process of mining, or unused biomass left in the process of harvesting. The things with which we come into contact, in all their compactness and neat presentation, actually have a "shadow" weight that sits unseen by most of us (Dauvergne, 2010). We could think of commodities as the "tips of icebergs," with much of their substance and effect lying unseen, but that would be misleading, since the histories of laptops, grilled sea bass, and everything else we consume are much more discontinuous than those of icebergs. They are perhaps better thought of in fluid terms, as a distilled essence composed of exchange value, picking up some material or substance (including embodied labour but also other embodied elements, such as water and carbon) and leaving some behind at different points along a disjoined web – a web which centers on two moments: you or I picking up lumber at the Home Depot or taking home a new outfit, both eventually to end up in some degraded form in a landfill or oceanic garbage patch; and profit being realized from surplus value accumulated along and around the web.

"Ten Ways to Reduce Your Impact"

So begins a bottomless well of internet-hosted lists about how you can bring about a perfectly sustainable, zero-waste world with easy changes to your consumption. These are all full of perfectly reasonable steps: stop using single-use plastics. Make your own health and beauty products. Shop in bulk using mason jars and cloth bags. Ride your bike. In addition to reducing the number of sea turtles with plastic straws jammed up their nostrils, these steps can apparently also make you happier, teach you new things, and improve your health. All to the good.

However, as we have been stressing, it is a terrible misapprehension to suggest that we can somehow separate consumer choices from the systems of which they are a part. There is a persistent gap between the increasingly eco-conscious consumer behaviours of a growing number of people in the mass-consumer societies of the North and the growing ecological damage wrought by the total scale of their consumption along with that of a rising consumer class in emerging economies such as China. So, while we scramble to avoid the withering judgement of our peers by carrying stainless steel water bottles (don't lose it – it is about as resource- and energy-intensive as 500 plastic bottles on a life-cycle assessment! [Goleman and Norris, 2009]), global capitalism swallows more and more raw materials: about three times as much now as in 1970. Figure 5.1 is a crude indicator of the amount of raw material that pours into the stuff we consume. In all of its brutal reductionism it conveys the sheer weight of our draw on the earth and its alarming rise.

Ecological footprint analysis similarly reveals that, in order to sustain the current scale and type of an average US resident's consumption, we need three additional earths (Global Footprint Network, 2019). While the wealthy countries of the Global North have driven the historic rise in consumption and its accompanying environmental tolls, the eyes of contemporary marketers keen to capture the next wave of consumer growth are turned largely to Asia. Following on the success of South Korea, where household consumption grew more than fivefold between 1990 and 2018, India and China are generally heralded as the next centers of middle-class consumption growth. The World Economic Forum, for example, predicts that consumer spending in India will increase from US$1.5 trillion in 2019

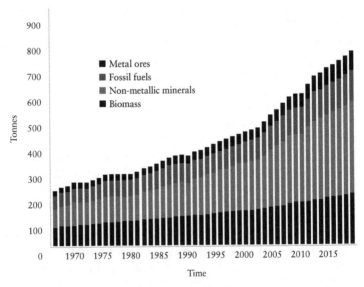

Figure 5.1 World domestic material consumption, 1970–2017, by material group

Source: Material Flows Analysis Portal: www.materialflows.net.

to $6 trillion by 2030 (World Economic Forum and Bain & Co., 2018). Their projections might be optimistic, given that growth rates have dipped since 2017 (Inani, 2020), but even taken with some caution, given the range of estimates on the proportion of the population that might count as "middle class" (Martin et al., 2013) and the uncertainty of growth rates following the coronavirus pandemic of 2020, Indian household consumption measured in constant 2010 US dollars has jumped threefold, from just under $400 per household to $1,200 in 2018. Income growth, poverty reduction and the high-consumption lifestyles of what the World Economic Forum has dubbed "liberalization's children" (those born after 1990) are projected to support rising consumption (World Economic Forum and Bain & Co., 2018). Already consumption is close to 60 percent of GDP in India and, while still relatively low (about 11 percent), household debt as a proportion of GDP is on the rise, suggesting a growing willingness to float consumer spending on credit. China's consumption, by comparison, is about 40 percent of GDP, but annual household consumption has grown from $665 to $3,154 – almost a fivefold increase, from 2000 to 2018 (World Bank, 2020). The per capita ecological footprint of these nations remains tiny relative to that of wealthy nations – China's weighed in at 3.39 global hectares, India's at 1.07 and Luxembourg's (the nation with the biggest footprint per capita) at 13.7. They are, however, likely to be the big growth centers for consumption in the coming years.

In order to get a grip on how consumption plays a distinctive role in environmental destruction, we can begin by looking at how many of the objects and experiences we so cheaply and blindly consume are cheap by virtue of somebody or something else paying for some of it.

Blindfolded

If there is one thing we can all credit capitalism with, it's providing an abundance of cheap commodities. These are snapped up with little thought about what processes brought this particular set of nested plastic mixing bowls or those smartphones before us to choose from (we'll deal with exceptions to this in chapter 7). Some – in fact, likely most – of those processes resulted in some non-consensual, uncompensated harm. This is not really how it's supposed to work in the ideal textbook model, of course. There shouldn't ideally be any costs or benefits from the transaction that spill out onto bystanders, like those sad sea birds you see getting washed by volunteers after an oil tanker crashes. Buyers and sellers should be fully aware, and absorb all, of the costs and benefits of their deals. Corporations, though, have a great many opportunities to push their costs onto somebody else – human or otherwise – and they do it as a matter of course and necessity.[1] Consumers might benefit from this in that they get cheaper stuff, though they frequently don't know why it's so cheap. The real losers are the sea birds. They pay a cost (a very dear one, from the sea bird point of view) for a transaction (in this case the purchase of oil) in which they had no part.

This is the old problem of externalities – benefits or costs that spill out beyond the parties to a contracted exchange. These can, of course, be positive. For example, when I pay a music streaming service and then proceed to play my impeccably curated collection at high volume, my neighbours get to enjoy that for no charge whatsoever. However, a great many externalities are negative. For example, when one of my neighbours purchases their music streaming service, and then plays their absolutely unbearable selection of "new country" hits at high volume, the whole neighbourhood suffers.

On a more significant scale, corporations almost never pay the full costs of their production, which means that consumers very rarely pay the full costs of consumption. Trace the history and future of pretty much any commodity you have purchased, and you'll find that, somewhere along the way, somebody or something is bearing an external cost.

Monetized estimates of the scale of this problem are always dependent on a lot of underlying assumptions, so their precision has to be taken with a lump of salt. However, such estimates can sometimes, as they were originally intended,

---

1 For an account of why this is necessary for firms, and the consequences for capital, for the environment and for politics, see O'Connor 1988).

signal the order of magnitude of a problem, acting as a kind of metaphor for the scale of destruction. An unreleased UN report suggested that the production costs externalized by the world's top 3,000 companies in 2008 tallied to somewhere in the neighbourhood of US$2.2 trillion (Jowitt, 2010). A valuation of the unpriced destruction of global "natural capital" came up with a total of US$7.3 trillion per year – about 13 percent of global GDP in 2009. More alarmingly, the report found that none of the sectors analyzed could actually bear these costs were they forced to pay them (Trucost, 2013). That is to say, the firms in these sectors owe their economic existence to the fact that they can slough a significant chunk of their production costs off on somebody or something else. This captures only the environmental side of things and, in the first example, only a narrow range of the total environmental damages. The very large costs of social reproduction – keeping children fed, households intact, communities together, education systems functioning, etc. – which are all vital to the functioning of businesses, are not included, so they are highly conservative estimates.

Some of this sloughing off of costs benefits the firms themselves and shows up as artificially inflated profit. Some of it, however, gets passed onto consumers, meaning that the prices we pay for most things don't actually cover the full costs of their production. Contemplate, for example, that icon of freedom, the automobile. Car buyers are largely unmotivated by a consideration of how significantly the car will degrade the planet by using up materials, energy, space, or the absorptive capacity of the oceans and atmosphere. They are, even as the planet heats, still quite happy to purchase many a high-carbon, light-duty truck or SUV, which accounted for a monstrous 69 percent of the US auto market in 2018 (Muller, 2019). Even in comparatively greener Europe, SUVs are the strongest growth segment in the auto market (International Council on Clean Transportation, 2019). And why not? After all, in their quest for a rugged (but urbane!) image, consumers are not confronted with the full costs of their decisions (unless their Armada happens to be swept away in an uninsured, climate-related flood event).

An effort at calculating the external costs of automobile operation alone (so excluding manufacture and disposal) across the EU suggested that the cars being driven there imposed between €258 billion and €373 billion per year, taking into account accidents, climate costs, air pollution and noise (Becker et al., 2012). That is a pretty hefty bill, delivered to other people (including people not yet born) who had nothing to do with the purchase. Costs to other species, such as those sad sea birds, are omitted. Car buyers and auto manufacturers are both, to some degree, getting a massive "bargain." Of course, for consumers, this bargain is on the individual scale and very short run. Taken as a collective, we will be facing at least some of these externalized costs in the medium and long run, in the form of bad air quality, oil spills, climate change, poorer health, more traffic fatalities and the occasional war. As the environmental justice literature tells us, however, it makes little sense to view these at the level of "collective consumers," since environmental hazards, like pollution, don't get experienced evenly (for a recent summary of the voluminous literature on this point, see Pellow, 2018). Environmental hazards, and the illness, death, dislocation and discomfort they cause, tend to pile up at the low end of the socio-economic gradient. This means that, if you are poor and/or racially marginalized, you are more likely to be paying for these externalities. For the manufacturers themselves, as corporate (or in some cases state-owned) entities, it's all surplus unless or until environmental degradation shows up in their supply costs (say, as a result of resource scarcity) (O'Connor, 1988).

What does all this mean for consumption? Some negative externalities arise directly from somebody's use of an item which generates an uncompensated harm to somebody else. Orthodox economists conceptualize this as a difference between the private benefit of the item to the consumer and the higher social cost resulting from the harm to others. These are theoretically solvable through taxation (called "Pigovian taxes" after economist A. C. Pigou). To take the example of the automobile, from above, we could add on separate taxes for the car's contribution to the social costs of accidents, air pollution, noise pollution, oil spills, urban sprawl, etc., and we would have successfully gotten the price of a car "right." Cars (and almost everything else) would, other things being equal, get more expensive, but, importantly, SUVs would get comparatively more expensive than electric cars, bicycles or public transit, as SUVs impose a much higher social cost. Similarly, large footprint, energy-inefficient shelter would be relatively more expensive than smaller, more efficient homes. There is also an approach to remedying the problem of externality, proposed initially by Ronald Coase ([1960] 2013). Rather than relying on government intervention through taxation, this approach relies on government intervention through the state's creation of markets in heretofore unmarketed goods and the corresponding need for government to assign private property rights to pretty much everything imaginable. That way, nothing fails to be captured through the price mechanism of the market. If the government assigns me a property right to a chunk of the atmosphere, then assumedly you and I can negotiate a rate of payment that will compensate me for your use of my chunk for the purposes of depositing nitrogen oxides from your tailpipe. Coase didn't think this would work very well for transactions involving very large numbers of people, a category that includes most environmental problems. However, its appeal among many economists remains.

Using the state to assign property rights and create markets, or using it to tax, establishes a monetary valuation for harms that can, in theory, overcome the problem of externality. However, consumers may not respond the same way to an externality-capturing increase in the price of a good as they would by being confronted with more immediate knowledge of the human and ecological consequences of its production. This is because, in the realm of consumption, the emotional appeal, the aesthetics and the style of an object matter. By some accounts, the ability to target emotional motivators is the best predictor of a company's success. If people "feel good" about a brand, they will pay more for it. Take, for example, the smartphones and laptops produced by the Apple corporation. Apple generates such emotional attachment and loyalty that people are willing to camp out on urban streets just to be early for the next model. People for some time (a fad now thankfully fading) staked out their identity as "Mac users," and social media are still full of people happy to spend their free time hawking the brand.

This warm emotional attachment – and Apple's impressive sales – might be more difficult to sustain were the externalities of smartphone and laptop production not hidden away in places such as Baotou, inner Mongolia, China. Baotou is a center of rare earth mineral extraction and refining. High-end electronics depend on these minerals to make things such as light-weight magnets, coloured glass, polished screens and electronic components. In 2015, a reporter began his article for the BBC as follows:

> From where I'm standing, the city-sized Baogang Steel and Rare Earth complex dominates the horizon, its endless cooling towers and chimneys reaching up into grey, washed-out sky. Between it and me, stretching into the distance, lies an artificial lake filled with a black, barely-liquid, toxic sludge. Dozens of pipes line the shore, churning out a torrent of thick, black, chemical waste from the refineries that surround the lake. The smell of sulphur and the roar of the pipes invades my senses. It feels like hell on Earth. (Maughan, 2015)

Baotou is a boom town built on the sacrifice of its local ecology and the health and well-being of its workers. The enormous toxic lake pictured in figure 5.2 is the hidden

Figure 5.2 This is your mobile phone
Images © Liam Young/Unknown Fields

flipside of the electronic commodities that consumers report loving. Whatever joy consumers experience in getting a hold of their new Apple product does not have to contend with this lake (or the various other environmental and labour-related horrors that lurk beneath the sleek exteriors). The strength of the Pigovian tax is that, when externalities like Baotou exist, even if people are not aware of the problems, they will be less likely to buy a more expensive, more externality filled phone. On the other hand, as with so much else in our world of exchange values, it continues to hide the social and environmental conditions of production.

Bloated: The Problem of Scale

What the question of externality fails to capture is the overarching problem of scale alluded to in figure 5.1. People have been using markets for exchange for millennia, with very little by way of growth until very recently. However, under capitalism, growth has expanded in an historically unprecedented manner.

As just one indicator of the restless growth of value (and the materials that embody some of it), consider the scale and rate of increase of the volume of stuff that moves across our oceans in search of either an intermediate production process or a retail shelf. Figure 5.3 shows a snapshot of the location of all cargo (lighter) and tanker (darker) vessels in the world.

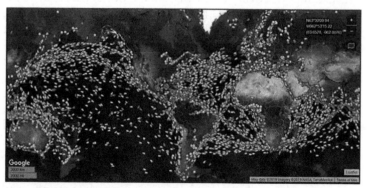

Figure 5.3 Marine cargo and tanker traffic, 23 May 2019
Source: www.marinetraffic.com.

These haul, from the point of production to the point of consumption, about 90 percent of final goods in the Global North (George, 2013). Depending on the state of the global economy, there are somewhere in the region of 100,000 ships on the sea at any moment, together carrying about 20 million containers. While shipping is incredibly carbon-efficient on a per-unit basis, compared to trucking or even rail, the scale of the industry is such that it produces around 2.8 percent of all greenhouse gas emissions globally (International Maritime Organization, 2014; United Nations Conference on Trade and Development, 2018: 6). Containerized trade is dominated by the routes running from East Asia to the large consumer markets of North America and Europe (ibid.: 13).

The bustling shipping industry, combined with the proliferation of free trade and investor protection deals, has allowed production to expand over the globe in search of cheap materials and labour, improving profitability and lowering the price consumers pay for anything from spatulas to flat screens. However, if we consider the weight of what it carries – the "material shells" of goods en route to making more of themselves so that yet more dots on the shipping map can appear next year – and the fact that it all passes relatively briefly through our homes en route yet again to a landfill, it should give us pause.

We discovered some time ago that the scale of our economy was beginning to put strains on the planetary systems that sustain us and the rest of life. We successfully pushed that discovery to the margins of our consciousness for a half-century as we in the Global North drove more cars, moved into bigger homes, and stuffed our closets. Now, in 2020, people are starting to wake up to the twin ecological disasters of biodiversity collapse and climate change and connecting these to the ongoing crisis of inequality.

Even as far back as 1848, John Stuart Mill tied economic growth to environmental degradation. He warned that, with the loss of "nature" to industrial expansion, the world and humanity would become deeply impoverished (Mill, 1909: 750–1). From Romantic reflections such as Mill's on the value of wild nature in the first half of the nineteenth century, concerns about the *desirability* of economic growth, and its uncertain connection to progress and improved human development transformed into a concern about its *feasibility*. Problems of material scarcity to sustain industrial production were a fairly constant theme in industrializing economies even in the first half of the 1900s. By 1951, these kinds of fears were widespread enough to prompt President Truman to strike the President's Materials Policy Commission (the Paley Commission), geared to generating policy proposals to ensure that material shortages threatened neither national security nor economic expansion.

The commission's final report, stressing the connection between growth and all things good, was titled *Resources for Freedom* and laid out the basic problem: "the consumption of almost all materials is expanding at compound rates and is thus pressing harder and harder against resources which, whatever else they may be doing, are not similarly expanding" (President's Materials Policy Commission, 1952: 1). However, the commission established a few articles of faith which guided its approach to the problem of materials scarcity. Crucially, it "share[d] the belief of the American people in the principle of Growth" (ibid.: 3). Scarcity, the commission argued, was a serious problem demanding public policy and planning, but continuing growth was not up for negotiation. The problem was to plan an adequate material supply to meet the needs of growth.

An attempt to question this appeared twenty years later. With the publication in 1972 of the Club of Rome's report *The Limits to Growth*, there emerged an environmentally tinged assessment of the possibility of perpetual growth, simultaneously pointing out the impossibility of infinite growth on a finite planet and exposing as myth the notion that growth will eradicate poverty and inequality. While the authors allow a Malthusian spectre a prominent place, highlighting population growth as the "greatest possible impediment to more equal distribution" (Meadows et al., 1972: 178), *Limits* questioned the widely shared assumption of progress through expansion. Its modelling of emergent resource scarcity under population and capital growth suggested that, at some unknown point – sooner rather than later, and likely within 100 years of the study – we would need to grapple at a global level with the tensions between the scale of our productive activities and the carrying capacity of the planet.

Many critiques have been levelled at *Limits*, accusing it of neglecting the boundless capacity of human inventiveness, ignoring price-driven substitution, or focusing overly on population growth. Indeed, establishing or asserting fixed biospheric limits to growth, as conceptualized by metrics such as carrying capacity, is very problematic. The ability of a place – even a planet – to support life is a product of distribution, of technique and technology, and of social–ecological relations (including decisions about what kinds of life count). However, much of the criticism levelled at the report neglects its nuance. As Donald Worster (2016: 166) argues, the argument was not strictly Malthusian, in that it neither justified poverty nor blamed the poor, nor did it fail to account for the discovery of new material reserves and efficiencies; further, it did not presume that the capacity to support life was fixed or focus just on productive scarcity but, rather, on the disruption of ecologies. Nonetheless, *Limits* became a target of sustained critique because its core idea, that growth is a phase rather than a permanent state, proved uncomfortable.

The authors and the publishers of *The Limits to Growth* were taken aback by the ferocity of their critics, surprised that their (in their own eyes, simple and obvious) claim about the impossibility of infinite growth should cause such a reaction. In the view of critics, allowing for limits would, variously, doom millions or billions to enduring poverty (which the report argued was more a factor of distribution of wealth than a shortage of production), bring non-material forms of progress to an end, open the door to authoritarianism, and result in gross violations of individual freedom (Worster, 2016). This last is of particular interest in our case, since the specific freedoms under threat were identified as choice over number of children and over the accumulation of possessions. Economics, at least in the mainstream of the discipline outlined in chapter 2, has a strong aversion to drawing lines around what is and isn't appropriate in terms of either quantity or quality of goods and services. Spending is spending, in this view, and it is tyranny to suggest that what one consumer wants is worthy (say, water) while what another wants is frivolous or destructive (say, a diamond). This has allowed the discipline to steer well clear of any taint of subjectivity or moralizing. It is this, in particular, that critics of *The Limits to Growth* found most troubling: that it would require us to abandon the notion that, eventually, there would be a chicken in every pot, a Tesla in every garage, and an unbounded universe of accessible consumer choice waiting at the click of the mouse for all of us. Poverty was, in their eyes, a problem arising from a lack of growth. *Limits*, on the other hand, suggested that the promise of boundless growth could no longer serve to rationalize existing, gross inequalities. The ferocity of its reception can be understood only if we recognize growth as a crucial component of contemporary capitalism, as well as its role in promising increased consumption for the poor without the undesirable recourse of taking from the rich. It also threatened the key narrative of consumer society: that human progress is about creating, owning and enjoying more stuff. The construction of longstanding ideals such as progress and freedom[2] in a quantitative register of "more" could not tolerate the imposition of physical limits (Passell et al., 1972; Roberts, 1975).

The need of businesses to expand and the associated cultural articulation of privatized, high-consumption lifestyles with freedom, progress and prosperity have brought us to a point of crisis. The spectre of *Limits* is with us once again, this time in the form of "planetary boundaries," whose crossing entails likely catastrophe. In 2009, a large team of scientists (Rockström et al., 2009) laid out the concept of a "safe operating space" for humanity, beyond which lay the possibility of "non-linear, abrupt environmental change within continental- to planetary-systems." Their paper attempted to resurrect the ecological core of the shop-worn notion of sustainability, using language strikingly reminiscent of the key theme from *Limits*: "The exponential growth

---

2 For an excellent treatment of the ideological role of growth, as well as its origins in political economy, see Dale, G. (2018) "'A Rising Tide Lifts Us All; Don't Rock the Boat!' Economic Growth and the Legitimation of Inequality," in G. H. Fagan and R. Munck (eds), *Handbook of Development and Social Change*. Cheltenham: Edward Elgar, pp. 151–72.

of human activities is raising concern that further pressure on the Earth System could destabilize critical biophysical systems and trigger abrupt or irreversible environmental changes that would be deleterious or even catastrophic for human well-being" (ibid.). The relevant limits are not simply about running out of stuff. They are about the disruption of ecological systems through withdrawal, addition and transformation. The research suggested initially that, of the nine identified systems, the safe boundaries of three had already been crossed, and subsequent research suggested this had increased to four (climate change, loss of biosphere integrity, land-system change and altered biogeochemical cycles) (Steffen et al., 2015). The Intergovernmental Panel on Climate Change has added yet further urgency to this situation, announcing that only if we are able to reduce carbon dioxide emissions by 45 percent by 2030, and get them down to zero by mid-century, are we likely to keep global net temperatures even within a 1.5 to 2.7 degree increase (IPCC, 2018).

So the question of whether perpetual growth is feasible within the confines of planetary boundaries has re-emerged, though it is only just beginning to have much by way of political force. The most salient proposals for addressing the climate emergency hang heavily not only on their compatibility with continued growth but on their ability to ramp growth up further. Hence the attachment of "New Deal" language to the process of transitioning to low carbon economies and the insistence on highlighting the growth and profit opportunities of climate mitigation and adaptation that are part and parcel of the Green New Deal, discussed in chapter 3. Growth remains a completely normalized, specific and, one might even suggest, non-negotiable target of policy. And, in order to keep that economic growth happening, consumption has to grow proportionally.

The stagnant incomes for most of the working class after 1980, highlighted in chapter 3, have made this more difficult and have also eroded to some extent the power of this narrative of growth-fuelled prosperity for all. Growth is sold less and less as desirable on the grounds that it will provide us all with a better and larger array of things and services from which to pick.[3] It is sold more and more as a necessary process to keep the wolf from the door. Growth is alleged to reduce the possibility that you will be without work, and thus without pay for the basics. For most in the mass-consumer societies, in the period of rising inequality, growth's appeal is based more in the fear of loss should it falter than on the promise of a better life.

Embedded Consumption and the Limits of Consumer Environmentalism

In trying to get to grips with the connection between our day-to-day consumption and the degradation of the planet's climatic stability and diversity of life, we have to look carefully at the extent to which consumers have a choice in the matter. Obviously, they have some, as the champions of consumerism argue. The choice between buying a gas-guzzling SUV and a small, efficient electric vehicle is, for the consumer with the cash to afford either, significantly within their hands. But, as we have seen in chapter 3, consumption is also a field of conflict under capitalism, and people's needs and desires are the objects of that struggle. And, as we'll see in chapter 6, consumption is as much about social communication, signalling, and seeking a measure of control and creativity within the narrow limits afforded us as it is about hedonistic self-gratification.

Another way of thinking about this is to understand that, while consumers do indeed opt for product A over product

---

3 The most recent exception we can find being Daniel Ben-Ami's *Ferraris for All: A Defense of Economic Progress* (Bristol: Policy Press, 2018), which argues that humans are not in any way bound by planetary limits, because we are very, very clever, and that human progress is well tracked by the accumulation of more stuff. While his title, he admits, is not to be taken literally, he does argue that growth is feasible, because of technological advance, and that it is desirable, because having more stuff – apparently without limit – is an unadulterated benefit. This despite the fact that he claims (http://archive.battleofideas.org.uk/2010/session_detail/4079) not to support consumerism.

B, this – and its environmental consequences – occurs within a heavily circumscribed set of structures. Practice theory, which we discussed briefly in chapter 1, has been useful in highlighting this. A great deal of our consumption is not aimed at showing off, setting ourselves apart from others, signalling belonging or expressing an identity. It is about getting from point A to point B, keeping from starvation, staying warm and dry, maintaining social relationships, staving off boredom, keeping healthy, learning things. As practice theory stresses, consumption is mostly something we do as part of other practices – cooking, driving, sporting, cleaning, etc. Practice theory also stresses that, through practices, we exercise discretion but do so within sets of motivations, understandings, procedures, rules and infrastructures that are part of a social order. Laws are an obvious example. There are many illegal forms of practice, which rules them out for a lot of people. Many others still engage with them, but that doesn't mean the rules don't affect their consumption-related practices. The consumption of illegal or controlled narcotics, for example, is highly circumscribed by law, profoundly shaping the experience of drug use. It is also structured by social norms within the community of users, understandings of dosage, preparation, quality and absorption, the availability of delivery devices, the physical spaces in which it occurs, the needs of the user in relation to their ability to satisfy them in alternative ways, cultural portrayals and functions of use, and a host of other factors apart from law. Practice theory enables us to situate our consumption – even the most humdrum forms that accompany everyday practices such as cleaning or getting to work – within a set of social structures. What, when, where, how and why we consume is in large part determined or at least conditioned by these social aspects of our practices.

A political economy framework stresses that these structures begin, at the most basic, with every firm's desire for expansion and the competitive requirement that firms profit. Only through a long and uncertain chain do consumers hold any sway over the environmental consequences of that production. We look at the extent of this power in chapter 7. The result is that the kinds of consumer goods available to us, whether purchased for material or cultural uses, exist because they are profitable to produce and sell. As we discussed in chapter 3, the profitable production and sale of commodities is not the only means through which to satisfy human needs and desires. Rather, capitalism's mode of allocating resources selects this form of need satisfaction. We can get water, food, housing, entertainment, safety, social interaction, joy or comfort through public provision, commons, expansive leisure time or any number of other means. The commodity form is the best option for capital (Manno, 2002).

In terms of how our consumption reorganizes nature, we also have to keep in view the historical fact that much of our consumption takes place within infrastructures bequeathed to us from the past (Shove and Warde, 2002): urban housing developments, transportation infrastructure, infrastructure for energy and water distribution, the complex and enormous industrial food system, building and other legal codes, and patterns of industrial development and trade (for example, the availability of building materials, household appliances or vehicles is not uniform across places). Opting out of many of these is extraordinarily difficult, if not impossible, outside of the construction of off-grid, self-sufficient homesteads and communities. The latter are few and far between and not cheap to build. There are increasingly options for dodging the most damaging aspects of industrial food production (particularly the increasing availability of vegetarian and vegan foods, the expansion of local farmers' markets, and some kinds of organic agriculture), but, even here, convenience and availability push the consumption of meat and highly processed foods.

To take just one example, the vast majority of North Americans unquestioningly accept that mobility requires driving a car. The former is inconceivable without the latter. As a result, we buy cars to get around even in cities, often despite being well aware that they are environmentally disastrous in all kinds of ways. But this choice is not the product of an autonomously generated consumer demand. Rather, as Gregory Shill (2019) has recently pointed out, in the US, legal codes "encourage" auto ownership to the point of requiring it by shouldering out any alternatives. Shill gives the example of single-family-only zoning, which separates commercial and residential activity, along with excluding apartments and multiplex dwellings from these neighbourhoods. The results are sprawling zones of large-lot homes connected by veins and arteries of roadways. Cities also legally enforce the provision of parking spaces – a massive subsidy to this privatized, individualized mode of high-consumption transportation – to the point at which Houston is estimated to have thirty parking spaces for every resident and about one-third of urban space in some cities is taken up by parking lots (Shill, 2019). US law has also been incredibly flexible on the establishment of speed limits (and high speeds make accidents more likely and walking and biking more difficult), as well as on enforcement and punishment of vehicle-related violations. Design standards have an exclusive focus on the safety of those inside the car as opposed to those outside of the car, as is the case in other jurisdictions. This makes it more and more dangerous to be a pedestrian (US pedestrian fatalities from car crashes increased by 46 percent between 2009 and 2016 (Lawrence et al., 2018)), and people are incentivized to buy larger and heavier vehicles like SUVs.

Perhaps most significant among the structures in which our consumption is embedded is the structure of the work day – both in its timing and in its substance. Our patterns of consumption are heavily beholden to the rigid regularity of the work day, its quantitative expansion, and the kinds of work that most of us engage in during "work hours." Much of this is simply about the increasing shortage of time we have to do things such as travel slowly (by bike or by foot, for example), prepare meals, mend or repair broken or torn objects, or even cultivate relationships. This lack of time encourages a convenience-oriented consumption of disposable goods which is environmentally destructive. Equally, it acts as an obstacle to the time-intensive process of finding out anything about the products we purchase: who made them, under what conditions, and with what consequences? In the next chapter, we'll look more at how the substance of our work lives is connected to our consumption.

Conclusion: Consumption as Ecological Practice

Even a cursory glance at the twin problems of externalities and limits to growth identified in this chapter should make it abundantly clear that relying on individual, voluntary consumption choices to solve environmental problems will always be grossly insufficient. Individual choice takes place in the context of an economic system, which, as currently structured, makes environmental choices increasingly unlikely and completely inadequate. They are unlikely because so many of the environmental costs are not included, and they are inadequate because, even if we managed to limp toward full cost pricing, the problem of the limits to growth would still loom over the scope of our environmental impact.

Even worse, the lack of full-cost pricing and the rejection of limits to growth are likely to persist because they are, at least in this moment, so beneficial to firms. An effective environmental politics in the face of an ecologically devastating scale and kind of consumption calls us to reorient struggle over how we spend our money away from choosing the stainless steel straw versus the plastic one – a politics that accords with the model of consumer sovereignty from chapter 2. Rather, a political economy of consumption pushes us to consciously reconnect with questions and politics about how we spend our time, over what priorities and whose interests will drive our economies, and about what kinds of constraints and enablers we can build to shift environmentally important practices of consumption – including the question of public versus private forms of consumption. This embraces ideological and normative constraints, to be sure, but we have to bear in mind that these aren't free-floating either. Norms and ideologies emerge in a dialectical relationship with experience and lived practice, the most straightforward and non-negotiable of which consist in the material reproduction of our existence – feeding, clothing, moving, sheltering, child-rearing: the nitty gritty of production and reproduction.

6
Consumption, Power and Liberation

We've made the case up until now that consumption should be understood as a terrain of conflict, and we've highlighted the need of businesses to recruit us into consuming, so that they can realize the profit potential of the stuff they make. On the other hand, we have people who want to live satisfying, fulfilled lives, who want good relationships with family, friends and communities, and who want to feel some measure of control over their lives. They want to connect with others, they want to be seen as of equal worth and, possibly, they want to be able to experience some measure of "freedom." Has the rise of commodity consumption – particularly in the post-war era in the Global North – delivered some of this? Has it been more successful in democratizing "the good life" and providing spaces for creativity, and for connection, than have other kinds of overtly political struggles for liberation? Even as we are engaged in a struggle over our free time and our disposable income with the businesses that would like us to buy their products, are we advancing a form of equality?

These questions form the crux of political economic analysis. While cultural studies that focus on the meanings fashioned by consumers in their encounters with brands and objects can be interesting in and of themselves, political economy's interest in this is whether the process of meaning-making through consumption serves as a means of emancipation or to thwart it. Political economy is about how social and political conflict within and around the production and reproduction of life impacts on people's abilities to meet their needs, fulfill their desires and realize their potential. This includes an analysis of how those needs and desires are generated but also of how capitalism structures the possibilities and the means for their fulfillment. We'll consider this by taking two divisions in society – class and gender – and exploring whether and how they are impacted by or in the realm of consumption. Within each of these categories, consumption is seen by some as a tool for exacerbating inequality and generating oppression and by others as a means through which inequality is reduced and oppression mitigated by opening a realm of freedom and independence to workers and to women. Much of this debate hinges on whether consumer choice is understood to be a real expression of liberation, or whether it provides the appearance of freedom while intensifying more deep-seated forms of conflict and subordination.

Class and Consumption

Consumption has been understood both as a set of practices designed to establish and highlight class difference and as a mechanism for eroding class difference. We'll look at the cases for both. The first of these, emerging from critics of consumerism, reveals how the acquisition, display and appreciation of particular kinds of objects serve to mark particular groups or individuals as belonging to a social elite. Historical accounts reveal how elites have long worked to set themselves apart from the riff-raff through fashion and accoutrements. As we saw in chapter 1, sumptuary laws, restricting certain kinds of clothes or decoration to certain social classes, were widespread. Under capitalism, of course, you are free to sport all the gold embroidery and lace cuffs you see fit. However, efforts at social distinction based on consumption haven't vanished.

Thorstein Veblen's ([1899] 1994) notion of conspicuous consumption suggested that the members of the "leisure class" – a group defined by its dissociation from any kind of productive labour – engage in ostentatious consumption strictly to make themselves visible as belonging to this group and to gain social esteem. This was an explicit poke in the eye to the economic models of chapter 2, which stressed rationally pursued, individually derived utility. Veblen argued that we needed to understand the consumption of objects in terms of what the possession of particular items (as well as participation in leisure pursuits) signalled to others. While it may seem as though this would limit the sphere of competitive consumption to an elite class, this is not the case. Those locked out of membership in the high-status leisure class are drawn into the consumer society through what Robert Frank (2013) would later call "expenditure cascades." Striving for prestige, members of lower-status groups emulate the consumption practices of those above them in the hierarchy – eventually recruiting all but the poorest into a process of competitive consumerism. Greater exposure to a wider range of other lifestyles, courtesy of the examples set by television programs, has also changed people's consumption "reference group," from those with whom they worked and who lived in their neighborhood, whose incomes are relatively similar, to people whose incomes are several times greater. The result is that there is upward pressure on what people consider to be necessities (Schor, 1998: 21).

The idea of conspicuous consumption is not hard to grasp in the era of social media and rising inequality. The "Rich Kids of Instagram" phenomenon, or the mercifully short-lived "flaunt your wealth challenge," in which people posed as though they had just fallen out of their high-end sports cars with their branded luxury possessions artfully scattered on the ground, are highly visible examples. Research also shows how this spills down to the non-elite, as the use of platforms such as Facebook has been found to elicit both narcissism and envy, each of which spurs on status-seeking conspicuous consumption (Taylor and Strutton, 2016). Websites such as Houzz showcase high-end home design, interiors and renovations, creating an endless sense of dissatisfaction concerning the present state of one's home and spurring expenditure cascades.

Some recent scholarship on the class distinctions of consumption has suggested that it has ceased to be an effective signal of elite status (Currid-Halkett, 2017) or that some among the very wealthy actively try to downplay their wealth (Sherman, 2018). However, while much of it takes place far from the eyes of the hoi-polloi, consumption among the rich remains far from moderate. The global "luxury" market is valued at about US$1.25 trillion annually (Avins, 2017), which is not small change. The rich occupy their own "parallel nation" (Frank, 2007), with its own health-care system, educational system, neighbourhoods, means of travel, clubs and insider-only status symbols. Stressed-out multi-millionaires frequently spend beyond even their inflated means in order to keep up with the Gateses and the Waltons. Few of them feel "financially secure," even as they cough up a half million in household staff costs and $600,000 on a wristwatch (ibid.). Veblen, it seems, still provides some solid theoretical material for understanding consumption.

A second question is not only whether consumption serves as a signalling device to distinguish members of a class but the extent to which aesthetic choices (tastes) in consumption also reinforce class power. Based on research undertaken with Parisians sixty-five years after Veblen, Pierre Bourdieu (1984) offered the most ambitious theory of how "lifestyle" intersected with class. He examined how the development and expression of "taste" (as expressed partly in consumption) both arose from and reproduced class differ-ences and inequalities. Aesthetic appreciation of objects, art, music or food is largely reflective of class position, according to Bourdieu, and this in turn demonstrates the fact that the upper classes have a more developed aesthetic disposition than lower classes. That is, "high status" people are more prepared to consider objects (even objects not legitimized as "art") in an aesthetic light – separating form from function and appreciating objects on the basis of form (Bourdieu, 1984; Lizardo and Skiles, 2015). This capacity is learned from childhood and forms one means of passing privilege from generation to generation. The upper classes, through their accumulation of this "cultural capital" – scarce knowledge, skills and dispositions – wield the ability to define good from bad taste, high from low culture, and even what can legitimately be considered from an aesthetic perspective. The lower classes largely accept this definition, arbitrary though it is, even though they often continue to embrace working-class culture. They might not, for example, try to appreciate ballet or opera, preferring to stick with familiar and traditional pursuits, but they nonetheless accept opera's and ballet's definition as high culture. Consumption, for Bourdieu, retains its role as a means of hardening class boundaries, as the acquisition and appreciation of specific kinds of objects corresponds to and signals one's appropriateness for a certain social position. Those who display appropriate taste as laid out in the elite definition of high and low culture, and instilled through class-specific processes of socialization, are better able to navigate social settings and relationships that provide access to jobs and opportunities. In Bourdieu's *Distinction*, consumption has an enduring structural association with social position, and the distinctive tastes developed among different classes make social mobility more difficult. Lifestyle is, according to Bourdieu, "perhaps one of the strongest barriers between the classes," because they simply can't stand one another's tastes. "The most intolerable thing, for those who regard themselves as the possessors of legitimate culture," says Bourdieu, "is the sacrilegious reuniting of tastes which taste dictates shall be separated" (1984: 56–7). Unlike with Veblen, then, everyone doesn't try to emulate the rich. Consumption, as a reflection of taste, however, functions both as a marker of class boundaries and to police them.

Finally, a longstanding critique of consumption is that it serves to pacify dominated populations and, in particular, to soften or deflect class conflict. Critics such as Marcuse saw consumption as an aspect of capitalism's totalizing control over our lives (in Gramsci's (1978) terms, it forms a pillar of hegemony, through which the majority provide their consent to be ruled). Here, the role of consumption in class divisions is perhaps most starkly expressed, with consumption acting not just as a marker and buttress of class boundaries (and of prestige) but as an active weapon in keeping the working class passive and distracted through the maintenance of an illusion that self-determination and freedom can be attained through consumer choice.

Consumers of the World, Express Yourselves!

Studies of consumption beginning (perhaps not coincidentally) in the late 1970s turned dramatically away from such gloomy critiques. Rather, they argued that, far from being a mollifying distraction or a self-aggrandizing display, consumption is a highly meaningful practice wrapped up with relationships, empowerment, resistance and creativity (Douglas and Isherwood, 1979; Hebidge, 1979, 1988; Miller, 1998). For Marxist-influenced writers such as Dick Hebidge, class divisions remained central to the analysis, as working-class youth subcultures rebelled against mass culture by "repositioning and recontextualizing commodities, by subverting their conventional uses and inventing new ones" (Hebidge, 1979: 102). For others, consumption was seen to offer an escape from class boundaries and limits (Twitchell, 1999). Still others, in apparent contrast to Bourdieu, have more recently argued that consumption doesn't have much correspondence with class but shows a remarkable fluidity between the cultures of the rich and the poor. What binds these scholars is their agreement that the significant thing about consumption is its symbolic, communicative nature and, in this vein (as symbol), its potential currency as a weapon in the negotiation of class relations.

Both Veblen and Bourdieu were subject to considerable critique as part of this shift. Veblen is accused of being interested more in condemning than in explaining consumption, and, indeed, his contempt for the leisure class, and for those he believes to be emulating the leisure class, is hard to miss. Colin Campbell ([1987] 2018), to take one prominent example, criticizes Veblen for ignoring possible reasons for consumption apart from emulation and status-seeking. He also calls into question whether there is any social agreement about what best represents social honour – so, by consuming conspicuously, one might not be sending the same signals to everyone, and some might seek status in frugality (ibid.: 96). Campbell is equally critical of arguments that suggest that consumption can be explained by firms' manipulation of our wants, as argued by Marcuse or Galbraith. This, in Campbell's view, treats consumers as overly passive, as "'empty' until 'injected' with wants" (ibid.: 87). In summary, the scolds such as Veblen, Adorno, Marcuse and Galbraith, all of whom suggest that in some way consumerism is wasteful and harmful, are critiqued as overly totalizing, dismissive of the intentionality and sophistication of consumers, monolithic in their understanding of consumer markets, and snobbishly elitist in their view of popular culture (Schor, 2007).

While acknowledging these critiques, however, Juliet Schor – a prominent defender of the critical tradition – points out that the grumpy critics of consumption had it right on many counts. People do consume, if not always, as a means of status-seeking. Culture is subject to pressures of industrial techniques, mass production and commodification. Advertisers and marketers do strive, and with some success, to associate commodities with our values and motivations, and also (*contra* Campbell) to alter those values and motivations in directions that make them more commodity-friendly but that don't make us happier (Schor, 2007).

Veblen's theory of status-oriented conspicuous consumption also appears to be conditionally supported by much research on contemporary consumption in the Global South (Nabi et al., 2019; Sun et al., 2017; Mathur, 2010). While status-based consumption was encouraged by colonial administrators and often flourished among local elites favouring the styles and products of colonizers (Arnould, 2011; Bauer, 2001), its diffusion has brought it into an articulation with existing local styles and tastes, as well as with moral and nationalist frameworks such as Confucianism in China, South Korea and Japan (Shepherd, 2011). Whether in a Western, local or hybrid form, it is clear that the incursion of new consumer goods, and acculturation campaigns to instruct people in their interpretation and use (Martin et al., 2013), is reorienting relations such that commodities assume a key role in defining people's aspirations and signalling status, honour and prestige. A great deal of retailers' optimism about the consumer potential of the rising middle classes of the Global South, such as in India (World Economic Forum and Bain & Co., 2018), rests not only on rising incomes but on a cultural transformation that is producing a population increasingly concerned with using consumption to demonstrate status and to negotiate social hierarchies and interpersonal relationships (Mathur, 2010).

Critics of Bourdieu, meanwhile, have argued that, while consumption may once have been a vehicle of class formation and reproduction, this is no longer the case. Upper-class consumption isn't predictably exclusive or snobby. High-status (affluent and educated) people instead compose a world of "cultural omnivores" who no longer pay attention to the status hierarchies of the objects they consume (Peterson and Kern, 1996). They embrace a diversity of cultural forms, both "highbrow" and popular – so they are just as likely to appreciate beer as they are fine wine. They are at the indie rock show as well as at the opera. As a result, consumption behaviours, according to this camp, are not predictable reflections of class position (Chan and Goldthorpe, 2007).

As Lizardo and Skiles (2015) argue, however, framing this in contrast to Bourdieu misunderstands him. Empirical research supporting the "omnivore" thesis actually confirms what Bourdieu himself found: that people with greater economic and cultural capital were more likely to embrace a wider array of objects as worthy of aesthetic contemplation, and, as you move down the social ladder, individuals are more likely to stick within a given definition of what is legitimately aesthetic. The playlists of the affluent will feature an eclectic mix that roams across genres, and those of the working class a less diverse mix of metal or country (Peterson and Kern, 1996).

There is, however, certainly no shortage of instances where the styles, taste and culture of subordinated classes and groups are "sacrilegiously reunited" with elite cultures and legitimized as "high status." And, while Bourdieu found that high-status individuals were more likely to embrace a diversity of objects as aesthetic even in the 1960s, what constitutes "acceptable" culture to middle and upper classes may be broadening over time. Gary Cross's (2000) history of consumption in the US, for example, shows that fears about the negative influence of working-class and black cultures (music, in particular) on white middle- and upper-class values were still high in the 1950s but had diminished by the mid-1960s, when economic and non-aesthetic class divisions had survived the upward influence of lower-class music and dress. Today, there is plenty of selective adoption of cultural and symbolic material from the lower ranks of the class hierarchy by the upper. The fact that luxury bag-maker Hermes has released a skateboard (hardly the kind of transportation or recreation we associate with the elite) or that the venerable elite fashion house Louis Vuitton collaborates with street label Supreme provide just two examples among many of such selective adoption.

However, the adoption of "culture from below," whether that is Elvis's (highly managed and controlled) smuggling of black American music into the parlours of middle- and upper-class homes or the influence of hip-hop and street culture on the entertainment and fashion of the rich, is always selective and normally purgative of any radical content. Pat Boone appropriated and sterilized black music in the late 1950s to make it acceptable for white middle-class youth and their parents (Cross, 2000: 107). While hip-hop's origins were rooted in black working-class resistance to the rising and racialized inequality of New York City, its commercial success and adoption by middle- and upper-class youth today involved the eradication of its radical messages (Huff, 2011). This process of careful selection remains the province of an economically and commercially influential upper class. That elites choose to adopt cultural material and styles from below doesn't change the fact that they have the power to define what is of value and significance, and that they have the money to acquire and display the "right" things. This was one of Bourdieu's main points: that power resides not just in economic capital but also in the correlated power of control over the symbolic world – the capacity to define what kinds of objects and practices are high status and which are low, and then to display an understanding of this order that distinguishes them from others. Bourdieu saw this conflict taking place in France in the 1960s mostly between two high-status groups – intellectuals, artists and "cultural producers" on one side and businessmen on the other – but the point remains that control over the definition of high and low culture is a resource of power. We might ask who has the balance of this power now? Who among us gets to define what is worthy of aesthetic appreciation? Are we now in the aesthetic hands of the influencers? If so, in whose hands are *they*?

From a political economy perspective, we also have to highlight the overarching fact that the creation of meaning in our lives through the acquisition of commodities – whatever they are, whatever meaning is assigned to them, and whoever does the assigning – is highly advantageous to businesses. They will not lose sleep at night if it is cheaply made hoodies and T-shirts that are propping up their profit lines rather than leather handbags and tailored blazers. If cultural materials from the poor, the marginalized or the subaltern were to represent a direct challenge to consumerism – an institutionalized social system of meaning which enlists the leisure time, income and life energy of the working class in the service of capital – then the businesses that profit from consumption would have cause for concern. But, overwhelmingly, subcultural styles from below are elevated into mainstream respectability precisely as a means of entrenching consumerism and propelling further consumption. While the risks of the cooptation of subcultures by business have been recognized by many, Thomas Frank expressed them well, suggesting that subcultural patterns of "rebel consumption," far from throwing up an obstacle to consumer recruitment, provide fuel for its acceleration. The rebel consumer, who attempts to express individuality and a "countercultural," even "anti-corporate," attitude through just the right assemblage of goods, keeps the machine running. As Frank puts it: "business is amassing great sums by charging admission to the ritual simulation of its own lynching" (1997: 153; see also Halnon, 2005).

So far, we've discussed whether consumption serves as a signal for status and class and to draw boundaries around class belonging. But does mass consumption change the centrality of class conflict or the arena in which it takes place? Does it serve to advantage either side in class conflict? Again, there are contrasting views on this. Some – Marcuse, for example – see consumerism as a tool to harden class boundaries. Others have suggested that consumption is in fact a more advantageous terrain of struggle for non-elites than either the workplace or the tilted playing field of electoral politics. Where workers occupy the low ground in the factory, the office and the electoral campaign, they hold the high ground in the shopping mall and the high street. As such, consumption has been seen as a vehicle for emancipatory class struggle (as well as struggles over patriarchy, which we cover below).

John Fiske, a major figure in media and cultural studies, argues that shopping is an effective "weapon of the weak" – a terrain of "tricks" played by the marginalized or underclasses. In their consumption practices, "the weak [use] the resources provided by the strong in their own interests, and to oppose the interests of those who provided the resources in the first place" (Fiske 2011: 19). While the "mass culture" of industrial capitalism puts on offer a huge variety of objects to be consumed in retail spaces, Fiske describes how youth occupy the spaces of consumption, such as malls, for their own cultural purposes, trying on or trying out things they have neither the intention nor the ability to purchase, socializing, and window-shopping for pleasure. He suggests that both commodities themselves and the spaces in which they are put on offer are symbolically turned back on their producers by savvy and ungovernable shoppers.

The argument, optimistic as it is, suffers from a number of problems. First, while Fiske suggests that teens, while hanging out at the mall, are "consuming images and space," this is not consumption as we define it. Nothing is actually being bought or used (Warde, 2017). Secondly, it turns out that a lot of stuff is actually being bought. Teens (today's "Gen Z") are a highly prized marketing demographic, partly because they are seen as style-setters, partly because they have heavy influence on family purchases, partly because firms know they will be big buyers in the future, and also because they carry some US$143 billion in their collective wallet (Fromm, 2018). Multiple pressures motivate and sustain this consumption. On the individual front, any kid in an industrialized nation's school system can tell you the social price of failing to live up to the dictates of rapidly evolving styles. Marketers work hard to prop up these social pressures, because a sustained failure to keep mass-produced commodities from being bought would be catastrophic for profitability.

Fiske's argument also misses much of the point by focusing on the subversive tricks kids play in the malls, looking at and trying out commodities without actually buying them. The key point is that they are there, being educated into consumerism, even if they aren't yet consuming. This is no less true of lives lived online than it was of lives lived at the mall.

Much of youth culture is geared toward being trained as consumers, which involves imagining future consumption as well as buying things in the moment. Youth inhabit a world in which – and are thereby taught that – prestige, status and meaning derive from commodity ownership (Deutsch and Theodorou, 2010). Deutsch and Theodorou argue that "within consumer culture ... adolescents' expectations for their future selves are likely to involve imagined patterns of consumption associated with their aspirations. These aspirations, in turn, are linked to youth's current and desired social class positioning and associated economic and personal power" (ibid.: 232).

Some go yet further than Fiske, to suggest that consumption has done for the working class what it could not do on its own, and broken the chains of class altogether. Consumption, they claim, "frees us from the strictures of social class" (Twitchell, 1999: 25–6). While material life used to be determined by lineage or by wealth, it now "evolves from a never-ending shifting of individual choice" (ibid.: 26).

Consumption has indeed acted historically as something of a damper on punctuated moments of sharp class conflict. The rise of middle-class wages and incomes in the post-war period, for example, served to build high-consumption lifestyles, with many of the trappings of wealth, below the level of the elites. This came along with an increasingly common expectation that things would continue endlessly to get better, in material terms: better houses, better cars and better lives as a result (Cross, 2000).

First it has to be acknowledged that the "democratization" of consumption is grossly exaggerated. There remain enormous differences in consumption across classes – even within wealthy societies. Secondly, while consumption may be experienced by the middle class as a realm of comparative freedom, this is the case only relative to the absolute dearth of agency or control they experience in the work world. Consumption has long been explicitly positioned as compensation for ceding control of the workplace. Frederick Taylor was a pioneer on this, suggesting that his engineered solutions to increasing productivity, while ruining the workplace as a site of human creativity and development, would allow both profit and wages to rise. "By 1912,"

Cross reports, "Taylor had articulated a social compromise. His solution rejected regulation and unions for an implicit bargain: labour would cede its claims over the workplace to management in exchange for high personally disposable income and shorter hours" (2000: 96). Freedom, in other words, would be found in the off-hours. As collective politics aimed at greater equality were pushed back (and ruthlessly so – see Gourevitch, 2015), a "consumers' democracy" was offered instead (see also Fones-Wolf, 1994; Fraser, 2015). This commoditized vision of the good life – derived not from creating a more equal society for all, or even from the collective life of kin or neighbourhood – was cemented during and immediately following World War II, promoted by unions which were purged of their radical organizers, and generously underwritten by the state through low-interest housing loans and the Interstate Highway Act. These enabled the great suburban migration, which, together with marketing, probably did more to increase consumption spending and consumerism in America than anything else (Cross, 2000). Working-class African Americans were largely excluded, but, for whites, the suburban "domestic nest was expected to be a refuge from and compensation for boring and stressful jobs" (ibid.: 97).

As Lizabeth Cohen (2003) shows in *A Consumers' Republic*, exclusion from the right to consume has formed the basis of important and successful struggles for equality (civil rights battles and feminist struggles in the US, for example). Restricted access to leisure and retail spaces, homeownership and credit were key dimensions of these collective struggles. However, in acknowledging this, Cohen also stresses that rising consumption and consumerism, far from acting to erase class boundaries, has in the long run served to exacerbate them. Cohen argues that the "citizen-consumer" of pre-World War II America, who still believed in the need for collective action in the public interest (even if they were not successful in winning it), gave way to the dominance of the "purchaser-consumer," for whom both duty and freedom were expressed exclusively through individual purchases.

Consumption and Gender

What, though, about gender? Has the increasing salience of consumption been a boon to feminists fighting for gender equality, or has it served the same role as it has in the case of class?

Second-wave feminism of the 1960s took a heavy swing at the complicity of advertising in the definition of femininity. In *The Feminine Mystique*, Betty Friedan (1963) dedicated a chapter to excoriating marketing's role in chaining women to domestic life, encouraging them to find fulfillment and expression in the home, largely through consumption. Though later criticized for focusing overly on the experience of middle-class white women (along with a lot of other early feminist critiques that concentrated on women's economic marginalization; Cole and Crossley, 2009), Friedan's analysis of business's very successful attempts to recruit this group as consumers was pivotal to her explanation as to why feminism as a social movement lost steam in the immediate post-war period. "The energy behind the feminist movement was too dynamic merely to have trickled dry; it must have been turned off, diverted, by something more powerful than that underestimated power of women" (Friedan, 1963: 197). That something, according to Friedan, was the fact that "the really important role that women serve as housewives is to buy more things for the house" (ibid.). Theorists of social reproduction, who highlight all of the many other kinds of unpaid work that women do, might well disagree (Federici, 2012; Luxton, 2017). However, Friedan's mining of consumer surveys conducted for industry are revealing of business's intentional construction of a feminine ideal rooted in domestic consumerism (see also Neve, 2009, 2010, on this process in early twentieth-century Munich). All that was to be preserved for men (creativity, a sense of meaning, agency, well-being and even sexual satisfaction) was to be granted to women in what Friedan claimed was an illusory form, through the purchase of things.

In this way, as noted in chapter 4, marketing and gendered consumerism ensure that women do much of the work required for the realization of surplus value through consumption. It is estimated that women account for somewhere around 80 percent of consumer spending decisions in the US. This isn't because women are richer than men, but because women, through the gendered division of labour, are more frequently assigned the work of household provisioning where needs are met primarily through shopping. Much of this is the kind of consumption to which Daniel Miller (1998) points in his study of working-class North London shoppers. Miller points out that the vast majority of consumption – and it is women who do almost all of it – is far from hedonistic and self-indulgent; rather, it is mundane and relational, conducted largely as a means of expressing love and care and performing sacrifice in the service of relationships. While Miller's purpose is to reject critiques of consumption that frame it as a selfishly individual and trivial pursuit, one can certainly see in his shoppers' accounts the feminized and privatized duty of household social reproduction. Similar themes are revealed in Bowen et al.'s (2019) rich accounts of American women's work in providing meals for their families, as they struggle to live up to idealized models of femininity, motherhood and the family meal. Shopping in this sense, while it may be a source of pleasure derived from knowing and helping satisfy the needs of loved ones, is still work.

The consumption characterized as "hedonistic" by its critics is celebrated by others as a form of self-expression, as a creative outlet and as a source of power for women. This dimension of gendered consumption becomes more historically salient with the increasing financial independence of women in the 1960s and 1970s (Stillerman, 2015), and its theorization rose to prominence as the cultural turn in sociology took hold beginning in the 1980s, focusing largely on the symbolic and identity-constituting elements of consumption.

Much of this focus is on the aesthetic aspects of consumption – with fashion coming under particular scrutiny. This is surely because fashion was one target of critics such as Veblen and because the aesthetic aspects of consumption were so important to Bourdieu's analysis. In specific contrast to Veblen's critique of consumerism as wasteful, indolent and compulsive, Elizabeth Wilson's *Adorned in Dreams* argues that "fashion is one among many forms of aesthetic creativity which make possible the exploration of alternatives" ([1985] 2003: 245), since fashion is both an art form and a symbolic social system. Wilson acknowledges that the fashion industry's production practices are a horror show of ruthless exploitation – largely of women. However, this aspect of feminist concern fades as Wilson argues that the symbolic power of fashion is mobilized for feminist resistance: "The pointlessness of fashion, what Veblen hated, is precisely what makes it valuable. It is in this marginalized area of the contingent, the decorative, the futile, that not simply a new aesthetic but a new cultural order may seed itself" (ibid.). Keeping up with and creating fashion (or other aesthetic practices) is not simply a hedonistic, self-absorbed practice, but it holds the potential for political dissent, including challenging women's subordination (much of which, Wilson notes, is symbolic, occurring through imagery and the representation of femininity).

Returning to Fiske's work on the powerful symbolic and cultural resistance available to working-class youth through shopping, we see a similar analysis applied to feminist struggles. Fiske sees women's engagement in shopping as a form of "semiotic guerrilla warfare" (Fiske, 1989: 19), by which he means that women (along with other consumers) take the materials given them by capitalism – control over the meaning and use of commodities, including their disfigurement (Fiske uses the example of people tearing their jeans as an expression of their capacity to make their own culture) – and turn them against the powerful. Both consumption itself and the spaces it requires are, for Fiske, potential tools for women's liberation. He juxtaposes the home, a longstanding realm of slavery and subordination for women to which patriarchy has attempted to consign them, and the mall, which is for Fiske a site of "all that is opposite," where women are public, empowered and free. The mall also serves to blur a central distinction of patriarchal society: that between public and private. Malls are seen as a space in between, in which women could gather and socialize. Fiske points out that department stores were the first public spaces, after the church, where women could legitimately go unaccompanied.

These victories, for Fiske, do occur in a context of alienation and the immersion of female lives in a commodity culture not of women's making. He acknowledges that our desire for commodities in all their diversity is a product of capitalism. Nonetheless, he argues that "the everyday culture of the oppressed takes the signs of that which oppresses them and uses them for its own purpose" (Fiske, 1992: 157). Women, he maintains, continue a centuries-long tradition of resistance to patriarchy by engaging in this appropriation of signs, making "guerrilla raids" through their everyday practices of consumption with the hope of eroding the ideological basis of male dominance over time. This emphasis on the power of culture and symbolic display as resistance grew through the 1990s, while the economic, materialist elements of the argument were eclipsed – as contained, for example in Baudrillard's ([1969] 1981) initial analysis of the economy of signs or in the earlier emphasis on the conditions of female textiles workers (McRobbie, 1997).

Symbols – including ads, of course, but also how consumers use and display the things they buy – are indeed powerful tools of struggle. If they weren't, we wouldn't have to worry about or celebrate the effects of advertising or marketing, or art, fashion, music or literature, on how we see the world. The representation of women in advertising and in other cultural media is a longstanding area of analysis within sociology, and also within media and cultural studies. So feminism has a tradition of resistance on this front, with early protests highlighting the portrayal of women primarily as sex objects or as domestic servants. The 1968 protests at the Miss America pageant, marked as a significant moment in contemporary feminism, used such objects as mops, lipstick and high heels thrown into a "freedom trash can" to make a point about women's oppression. These protests also tied women's oppression to other forms such as racism (Miss America had rules explicitly restricting the contest to whites and did not have a black winner until 1983) and US imperialism. A strong current of 1960s and 1970s feminists aligned themselves with struggles for socialism and to the peace movement. This second-wave feminism, while clearly cognizant of the importance of the symbolic, focused heavily on economic and political realms – struggling for equal pay, for a better distribution and valuation of social reproduction work, and for greater political power.

Feminism's third wave turned more heavily – almost exclusively – toward the symbolic, though in a different way. While marked by some real and some mythologized differences from the second wave (Snyder, 2008), third-wave feminism turned from lambasting the sexualization of women in culture and media, and their construction as objects of male desire, to a strategy in line with the one outlined by Fiske: taking imagery, objects and symbols from within the dominant culture and discursively reappropriating them. According to one seminal text on the subject, the third wave "encompasses the tabooed symbols of women's feminine enculturation – Barbie dolls, makeup, fashion magazines, high heels – and says using them isn't shorthand for 'we've been duped.' Using makeup isn't a sign of our sway to the marketplace and the male gaze; it can be sexy, campy, ironic, or simply decorating ourselves without the loaded issues" (quoted ibid: 179). Here, consumption and consumerism are celebrated as avenues of pleasure, fun, creativity, sexuality.

Additionally, they are seen as empowering for women, as everyday resistance. Toe-nail painting, cooking and getting dressed are all, in this view, feminist acts (Snyder, 2008: 186). Rejecting not only organizing but also the goal of mass social movement, third-wave feminism jettisons the notion of a common women's experience and, along with it, any idea of universality (a shared understanding of well-being or shared mode of subordination). What is left is a struggle for individual liberation, achieved through choice, constructed largely along consumerist lines. The beauty industry, for example, continues to be a topic of critique, as third wavers highlight the gap between the industry's representations of women and women's day-to-day lives. But that industry is also both a source of pleasure and a toolbox for creative (even subversive) self-expression. One critic argues that the third wave contains (though not without contest) a politics in which "any choice that fulfills a woman's need or desire is feminist" (ibid.: 189). Breast augmentation, to take an example raised by Zeisler (2006), can be seen as a means of individual liberation – and thus as feminist – for somebody who suffers from insecurity within a social context that rewards a particular feminine ideal.

Once political expression and practice become understood as a matter of fulfilling individual need or desire, we are in a lot of trouble. To "fulfill" is to take the forces that condition our wants and desires as given. Under capitalism, those needs and desires are highly attuned and responsive to the worlds of advertising, and they are sure to be met through a profitable commodity form. Under patriarchy, they are highly likely to be conditioned by gendered constructions of appropriate social roles, behaviours and aesthetics which have primarily benefited men (Milestone and Meyer, 2012).

A project of liberation must always grapple, as many traditions of feminism have done and continue to do, with the connections between individual decisions and the overarching social context in which those decisions are made. As Summer Wood (2006) asks, what implications do "liberatory" consumer choices have for the perpetuation of patriarchal relations broadly? As she laments,

> "It's my choice" has become synonymous with "It's a feminist thing to do" – or, perhaps more precisely, "It is antifeminist to criticize my decision." The result has been ... an often misguided application of feminist ideology to consumer imperatives, invoked not only for the right to decide whether to terminate a pregnancy (the initial emphasis on "choice" among feminists) but also for the right to buy all manner of products marketed to women, from cigarettes to antidepressants to frozen diet pizzas. (Ibid.: 146).

These two versions of "choice" represent markedly different forms of politics. The battle for reproductive choice launched and sustained a universalist claim for women's control over their own bodies, a struggle which benefits every woman around the world, including and perhaps especially the poor, by giving them the right to terminate a pregnancy. It is a victory won (though not definitively) on the back of decades of collective struggle that applies across boundaries of income and race. It is "Other-oriented" and solidaristic in a way that consumer forms of political protest are not.

In the case of both class and gender, we have to ask whether forms of expression deemed "liberatory" come at the cost of other lives – human and non-human. Even granting that some consumption is not self-regarding but carried out as a practice of love and care for family members, the implications of this consumption – both in quantity and in kind – reach well beyond the household and may well reproduce and reinforce all kinds of oppressions. Put slightly differently, "fulfillment" within capitalism is always of an anxious, temporary variety. As the biologist Robin Wall Kimmerer argues in *Braiding Sweetgrass*, while reflecting on the radical nature of indigenous practices of showing gratitude for the plenitude of nature, "in a consumer society, contentment is a radical proposition. Recognizing abundance rather than scarcity undermines an economy that thrives by creating unmet desires. Gratitude cultivates an ethic of fullness, but the economy needs emptiness" (Kimmerer, 2013: 111). Capitalism and patriarchy together provide the parameters of what fulfillment looks like and the means through which it is sought. And fulfillment through the form of the capitalist commodity almost inevitably comes at the cost of some Other's diminishment.

Firms, in their recruitment of both women and men as consumers via fostering dissatisfaction and "emptiness," make liberal use of gendered symbolism, and there is no doubt that this is both highly effective and damaging. While representations of masculinity play a huge role in advertising, and men are undoubtedly recruited to consume through tropes of "the breadwinner," of ruggedness, action and rebelliousness (Stillerman, 2015), women are doubly targeted in this process. First, subordinate and sexualized images of women are used to sell to men, reinforcing the patriarchal positioning of women primarily as objects of pleasure for men. Secondly, advertising and sales do not thrive on providing people with satisfaction and contentment but must perpetually be creating the opposite, and they do so ferociously in the case of women.

Marketing famously operates by playing on our senses of insecurity, anxiety and fear – many of which are fed by gendered expectations of body, dress and comportment. Angela McRobbie (2015) has written about the way that increasing resistance to more broadly acknowledged forms of gender inequalities – from routinized sexual harassment and violence to gender-segregated toy aisles – is channelled into an individualized form of feminism at whose core is an ultimately unmanageable quest for "the perfect." While the perfect does involve career success as one of its dimensions – the kind of individualized feminism characteristic of the advice of Facebook's chief operating officer Sheryl Sandberg to "lean in" – McRobbie argues that

> The perfect relies … most fully on restoring traditional femininity, which means that female competition is inscribed within specific horizons of value relating to husbands, work partners and boyfriends, family and home, motherhood and maternity. Reduced to journalistic clichés, this comes to be known as "having it all." The perfect thus comes to stand for the relationship between successful domesticity and successful sexuality. (Ibid.: 7)

This drive to competitively demonstrate "having it all" occurs through the family, the body and through consumption. Social media – ultimately a set of platforms upon which we make ourselves visible and legible for marketers – are another prominent vehicle for this competition among middle- and working-class women and girls. As women internalize the practice of measuring and monitoring their own progress toward the perfect, this progress is both marked and supported through consumption – Fitbits, kitchen appliances, children's and women's fashion, health foods, yoga accoutrements, vacations, etc.

While commodities are indeed symbolically monkeywrenched and subversively appropriated by consumers, all those trucker hats, "mom jeans," and Pabst Blue Ribbon beers contribute to firms' profitable bottom line, no matter how ironic their consumption. For the most part, patriarchal relations are either untouched or reinforced through the sales effort.

Just as the working class was forced to redirect its energy from an attempt to gain control over the workplace and over political life and into an individualist accommodation with capitalism through "consumer freedom," so feminism faces a similar pressure under patriarchal capitalism. What is jeopardized is as central to earlier versions of feminism as it was for working-class struggles for liberation: that is, the struggle for broad equality. Feminist politics has not just been about freeing women from patriarchy – let alone about freeing women to participate on even terms with men in a competitive rat race. It has held at its core the mission of building a better, more equal world for everybody.

Feminist politics after the third wave have turned aggressively back toward this, through the Women's March on Washington marking the inauguration of President Trump in 2016, the explosion of the #MeToo movement and the wave of protests launched in 2020 (with earlier antecedents) from Latin America. All of these point out the political and social context in which sexual violence occurs: one in which male domination is normalized, and in which legal structures and law enforcement are complicit in enabling and excusing gender-based violence. These are struggles that return to the universalist claims about women's fundamental equality and a collective refusal to be subjugated.

Feminism is at its heart about the alleviation of all forms of oppression. As Cole and Crossley (2009) argue, embracing consumption as a means of liberation is fundamentally contrary to that objective: "consumerism as the cultural logic of capitalism," they argue, "is the ideological and practical means to reproducing hegemonic domination of the exploitative and oppressive system of global capitalism. Although feminist identities are multi-dimensional, nuanced, and oftentimes individualist, consumption in a capitalist context is a fundamentally un-feminist thing."

7
Shopping Police

"LOVE this app!!" exclaims an online reviewer of the smartphone app Buycott. Buycott is one of several apps that enable users to scan barcodes and find out if a product or company aligns with their morals. "Changed my life," the review continues, "by EASILY giving me Real [sic] power to choose who I support with my dollars. The only way these companies will understand it."

Buycott and similar apps are the twenty-first-century version of a kind of political action that has been around for a long time. Embracing the power of consumer choice, seen as a lever for changing corporate behaviour, production practices or even laws, "political consumerism" (also talked about as ethical consumerism or consumer activism) is now a routine part of the marketplace.

As our reviewer above revealed, the idea is to enable shoppers to dig below the surface of the commodity to take account of how the thing was made, by whom, under what conditions, and with what effects for humans and non-humans. Once those normally obscure data are part of the decision mix, consumers are empowered to send an ethical message to producers using the only language that businesses are alleged to understand: market demand. This chapter looks at political consumerism both as a powerful lever for pressure and as a concession to the increasingly widely accepted notion that we are first and foremost consumers – including in our political lives.

Shopping as Power

Political action on the basis of a consumer identity was a
prominent form of activism in the early and mid-twentieth
century (McCracken, 1987; Trentmann, 2016; Guard, 2019).
Groups organized themselves as consumers and worked
politically to protect working-class families from unsafe
and unhealthy goods, price gouging, and other unsavoury
business practices, as well as, at times, trying to reinforce
other working-class struggles (Hilton, 2003; Glickman,
2009). The political consumerism we look at in this chapter
turns this previous consumer movement on its head. Rather
than using the power of collective action and of the state
to protect consumers, contemporary political consumerism
attempts to use the power of individuals' market behaviour
to induce social change. Political consumerism also does not
focus primarily on collective action or state protection in the
interests of consumers themselves – though there are elements
of self-protection in some consumer movements related to
food safety. More frequently, it uses the act of consumption as
a tactic for advancing the interests of someone or something
else – coffee farmers, dolphins, rainforests. The rise of
political consumerism beginning in the 1980s and booming
in the mid-1990s and early 2000s comes on the heels of
the conservative-corporate defeat of government consumer
protections (Glickman, 2009) and along with the roll-back
of the state's environmental and labour protective functions
that accompanied flexible accumulation.

Moralists have been asking consumers to pay attention to
the ethics of consumption for at least a couple of centuries.
Consider the words of John Ruskin, writing in the late 1800s:
"In all buying, consider first, what condition of existence you
cause in the production of what you buy; secondly, whether
the sum you have paid is just to the producer, and in due
proportion, lodged in his hands" (Ruskin and Wilmer, [1860]
1986). Ruskin is asking consumers to regulate their shopping
based on a very broad consideration of its effects – something
that, with the distancing of production and consumption
through trade and the increasing complexity of production
processes, has become infinitely more complex. Nonetheless,

the continuities between early and contemporary political consumerism are remarkable. The two images shown in figure 7.1, though they were produced two centuries apart, are both part of anti-slavery consumer campaigns using labels to advertise products that are free from slave labour. While still a routine part of many industries, slavery has been the target of consumer campaigns in the United States going back to the "free-produce movement" initiated by Quaker abolitionists in the 1820s, taking inspiration from consumer campaigns focused on sugar in Great Britain in the 1790s (Glickman, 2004). Both the original consumer movements and their contemporary versions hold a model of social change with consumer choice at its center. "If there were no consumers of slave-produce," the Quaker campaign claimed, "there would be no slaves" (ibid.: 894).

There is also, of course, the longstanding tool of the boycott, which is the flipside of labelling. The history of the boycott is actually entangled with other forms of political protest, and, at its beginnings, it was more about the complete isolation and shunning of individuals deemed to be stepping outside of legitimate norms. It was not just a market action, being rooted in a much broader social isolation; a great deal of its enforcement was certainly illegal, and it was backed by a communally sanctioned threat of violence (Feldman, 2019).

Contemporary boycotts are much narrower affairs: they stick largely to legal means, and they are understood as a consumer-based protest occurring through market channels.

Figure 7.1 Anti-slavery consumer labels, 1820 and 2019

Source: www.endslaverynow.org/act/buy-slave-free;   photograph   by Andreas   Praefke,   2011,   https://commons.wikimedia.org/wiki/File: East_India_Sugar_not_made_by_Slaves_Glass_sugar_bowl_BM.jpg.

They are a tool for activists from across the political spectrum. Today's caricature of the "latte liberal," smugly sipping their fair-trade, locally roasted, organic coffee, positions consumer activism as a liberal (in the contemporary US sense of the word) field. Indeed, the boycott was a staple part of the repertoire of labour and civil rights activists, both associated with the left. But boycotts have been and continue to be used by conservative groups as well. In the US during the nineteenth century, Southern whites called for boycotts of Northern goods as part of their battle to maintain slavery and segregation. More recently, conservative Christian groups have targeted a handful of multinational corporations, calling for boycotts in protest of their diversity policies and public support for LGBTQ rights (Heldman, 2017: 161–2). Sometimes, the politics are difficult to locate cleanly on this spectrum, as when fights for decent employment conditions are carried out through boycotts that mobilize xenophobic, nationalist or racist rhetorics.

Boycotts have found fertile ground as a tactic in the US, since they are perceived as a manifestation of consumer freedom and because of their early association with the Revolutionary War (the Americans called for a boycott of British goods). However, they have also been historically viewed as a form of unfair collective tyranny, as a foreign tactic unsuitable to American society, as a form of illegal conspiracy, and as an extreme form of mercurial mob power. The potential power of the boycott was deeply feared, with *Harper's Magazine* describing it in 1886 as "a new form of terrorism" that "seeks to destroy its victims, not by the guillotine or the dagger, but by depriving them of the means of support" (quoted in Glickman, 2009: 138). The class dynamics suggested by the evocation of the guillotine here are clear. Boycotters were depicted as a capricious, destructive force, capable of bringing capital and industry to its knees (ibid.: 137).

Despite efforts to stamp it out as a practice, however, the boycott has endured and has spawned similar forms of resistance to particular business practices or means for consumers to "hit back" at misbehaving brands (Kahr et al., 2016). Shopping, then, has a long history of being deliberately entangled in politics. The line between a realm for citizenship and a realm for consumers is blurry. Along with the strike, the demonstration, the pamphlet and the blockade, the boycott has been a feature of social conflict, and, while companies work to recruit people to take the final step in the realization of surplus, social movements attempt simultaneously to recruit them as moral enforcers.

Easy on the Surface, Hard Underneath

Political consumerism makes both an easy and a hard ask of its participants. The easy part is to make different choices while shopping. If you can afford it, taking this form of political action is straightforward. Move 5 feet down the aisle in your local supermarket, away from the giant tin of Folgers coffee, and pluck one of the many varieties of fairtrade coffee off the shelf. Political consumerism pragmatically engages with people where they already are – in the mall or the supermarket – rather than trying to get them out in the streets. It offers a straightforward, legal, anonymous, non-disruptive and relatively painless means of flexing your muscles, providing a sense that, in choosing correctly, you are making effective change. Political consumerism attempts to seize on our successfully constructed identity as consumers and to turn it toward political ends. The supermarket becomes a giant ballot box, with ballots weighted heavily in proportion to the size of one's bank account.

If it is to become more than just following the advice of Fox News pundits or Oxfam activists to avoid this product and instead gravitate to that one, or of simply believing in any product packaging that makes a claim about being "green" or "fair," then political consumerism's ask of its participants gets much harder. The difficulty appears in figuring out which objects align with which political aims. Political consumerism asks people to confront and overcome commodity fetishism, individually, in their role as shoppers (with assistance from apps such as Buycott, shopping guides from endslaverynow.org, or certificates such as Fairtrade). As we discussed in chapter 3, consumers encounter commodities as inscrutable objects. We don't know much about their provenance, about who made them, under what conditions, using what materials, with what consequences. Every commodity is a proverbial black box. We are encouraged to understand the commodity purely in the ways it is presented to us by product designers, branding professionals and retailers. Products do carry meaning beyond their objective form and function, but only very rarely does that meaning have anything to do with the labour that produced them or the environmental transformations brought about by their production. Political consumerism asks people to look under the hood, and even under the hood of the hood, to see the processes that are hidden in and by the commodity. It then asks them to find a commodity whose production does some good, or at least does less damage, and to vote for that product at the checkout.

Terror of the CEO?

Political consumers go through this work, with varying degrees of diligence, based on the belief that their choices will register with businesses and force them to mend their ways. Does this kind of market-mediated political action make a difference?

Some high-profile historical boycotts suggest that they can be effective in bringing about change. In the 1960s, the National Farm Workers' Association – which later became the United Farm Workers (UFW) – launched a boycott of non-union grapes, and millions of shoppers joined in. The boycott played a major role in getting the first collective agreements signed by the UFW. In the 1980s, an international boycott of South African products and tourism, while likely not the only factor – or even the most important one (Alsheh, 2019) – contributed meaningfully to the eventual dismantling of the racist apartheid system.

However, for each visibly successful and highly supported boycott, there are likely hundreds that fail to attract much solidarity. Claims of wild success by boycott organizers and of dismal failure by their corporate targets are both suspect and subject to contesting definitions of success. However, boycotts today operate through a fundamentally financial logic. The intent is to press for change by threatening (or effecting) losses in revenue or share value. If a boycott is to be successful, this threat has to be credible, or actually realized. Quantitative research on the change in sales or on corporate value (share prices) following a boycott tries to shine a more objective light on whether this is the case, and studies find that boycotts do tend to take a financial toll on targets (Pandya and Venkatesan, 2016; Pruitt and Friedman, 1986; Tomlin, 2019). Whether that toll is sufficient to get firms to take on costly reforms which address the problem, or to engage in a public relations campaign to polish their image and restore their brand, remains a murky question, still debated within activist circles.

Research on labelling also leaves us uncertain as to its effectiveness. Early work on the efficacy of labels by Bird and Robinson (1972) suggested that the union label campaign – usually noted as one of the more successful early labels – had very little effect on either union or non-union members' purchasing. Today, however, ethical labels are much more a part of the consumer landscape than they were before the 1990s. Not only is consumer labelling becoming more common as a means of pushing better business practices, but consumers are engaging with them in larger numbers. Taking just one example, the widely recognized fair-trade labels, measured by commercial indicators, have been a massive success. From its extremely humble beginnings and early years, characterized by informal trading out of car trunks, churches and charity shops (Hudson et al., 2013), Fairtrade has boomed by publicizing the exploitative and unsustainable production of such everyday commodities as coffee, tea, sugar, cocoa and wine and offering products that pledge to do better. Both the variety of commodities bearing the Fairtrade label and the number of organizations in each sector being licensed as Fairtrade producers have grown rapidly over the past two or three decades (Fairtrade International, 2019).

Meanwhile, the green frog of the Rainforest Alliance (RA) appears on thousands of products, ranging from coffee and cocoa to guitars, lumber, furniture and office supplies. Intended to reflect the product's sustainable origins, including both environmental and labour standards, the RA seal is a common sight for most shoppers in the Global North. The Forest Stewardship Council (FSC), which certifies sustainably sourced wood and paper products, and the Marine Stewardship Council, which certifies sustainable seafood, are also increasingly visible at the hardware store or supermarket. The success of these labels has occurred within a proliferation of competing labels, all signalling some dimension of alleged ethical production. As of 2019, the database kept by Ecolabels Index covers 463 ecolabels from around the world in twenty-six industry sectors. A proliferation of marketing literature on corporate social responsibility, on how best to head off brand-negative consumer activism, and on how to engage more discriminating ethical consumers suggests that political consumerism is beginning to have an impact at the level of corporate governance – even if it is only to develop emergency battle plans when boycotts or brand vandalism loom (see, for example, Grynbaum and Maheshwari, 2017; Guckian et al., 2017).

Saviour of the Worker, Farmer or Forest?

While the boom in labels and the commercial success and growth of individual labelling initiatives such as Fairtrade appear promising, it is not so clear that they are making much headway in dealing with their environmental and social objectives. Fairtrade, for example, was established with the expressed goal of alleviating the poverty of producers in the Global South whose labour is responsible for our daily food and drink.

Yet Fairtrade, despite its massive expansion, is not single-handedly bringing farmers out of poverty. Research on the impact of Fairtrade on producers suggests that, while more and more farmers and workers are producing under fair-trade conditions, their incomes are only modestly improved, and many of them remain in poverty (Jaffee, 2007; Fort and Ruben, 2009; Jena and Grote, 2017). Most studies do show that fair trade enhances security of land ownership or access, improves access to credit, and stabilizes price fluctuations, while giving a small boost to income (Hudson et al., 2013; Dammert and Mohan, 2015). In some instances, it provides social and political benefits such as improved organizational capacity for cooperatives and a sense of democratic control on the part of farmers, but these benefits are uneven across places and co-ops (Hudson et al., 2013). And these benefits go only to the very small portion of producers who sell their products under the Fairtrade label in the very small number of products in which Fairtrade labels exist.

Fairtrade is not alone in its less than stellar progress in tackling through the market activity of consumers what is, after all, a highly complex, longstanding and structurally entrenched problem. Despite the ubiquity of the RA green frog, rainforests remain under threat, agriculture remains largely unsustainable, and biodiversity is in steep decline. Consumer power does not appear to be transforming production practices in the service of equality, poverty eradication or ecological sustainability. This is not to say that labelling initiatives are useless, or that consumers are being swindled by empty appeals to their conscience. It is to say that political consumerism on its own is not up to the job – a claim with which advocates and pioneers of Fairtrade and other labelling initiatives would likely agree. If this were simply about continuing to scale up the coverage of such schemes as RA certification, Marine Stewardship and Forest Stewardship councils or Fairtrade, then we could declare political consumerism a highly promising, but unfinished project of regulating capitalism. However, there are some contradictions that come along with relying on consumers to address the poverty, injustice and environmental degradation that are part of the things they consume. Because of this, it may not simply be a matter of getting more shoppers to join in. In fact, doing so might undermine the force of political consumerism. We use the example of Fairtrade's history to illustrate this.

Many apparently ethical labels are just another form of marketing, with no substantive difference in the process of production, conditions of labour, or environmental impact of the thing bearing the label. However, of all the major labelling initiatives, Fairtrade is a best-case example. It was started by activists driven by a social justice mission, not by an industry group or a corporation trying to cash in on a niche market. From the outset it stressed partnership and cooperation across the North–South, consumer–producer divide, including (though not perfectly) in its organizational structure. It relies on rigorous third-party certification and the development of standards across a broad cross-section of issues (organizational requirements, labour standards, minimum prices, duration of contracts, environmental standards, gender equity, etc.). So, in looking at Fairtrade, we hope to give political consumerism its best possible assessment.

Too Much to Bear: The Trials and Tribulations of a Label

Fairtrade started small, and early on it used different ways of conveying the ethical content of the products that moved through its exchange networks. The first "fair-trade" product was lace from a Puerto Rican sewing circle, transported to Akron, Ohio, in the trunk of Edna Ruth Byler's car in 1946 (Fairtrade Federation, n.d.). Political consumerism at this stage relied on a customer base with a shared system of norms and values and on information that flowed through networks of solidarity, charity and religion. People purchased fair-trade goods, particularly in the very early years, because they knew somebody or were associated with an organization that was using the sale of craft goods to assist Southern producers. You had to be "in the know" to get your hands on fairly traded goods. They weren't found in stores. You had to be tapped into the particular network of individuals and organizations, which came later to be collectively known as alternative trade organizations (ATOs). Even when shops selling fair-trade goods began to open – there were thousands of these so-called world shops in Europe by the 1980s (Raynolds and Long, 2007: 16) and a smattering in North America – they were generally patronized by customers who were linked in to these networks. So fair trade was at the outset connected organically to social groups committed either to charity or to justice.

Equally informal was the basis of the claim of "fairness" that is now the core message of the Fairtrade labels. Early on in the fair-trade movement's history, the claim that trade was "fair" or in some other sense helpful to the producers was backed by nothing more than the word of the importer. In 1970 it was a trust relationship or a belief that enabled customers to ship off a cheque to a catalogue-based ATO or to make a purchase in a world shop.

The problem with networks of trust, however, is that they can only extend so far. Eventually, somebody at a certain distance from the core of the network is going to pause and say, "But how do I know that the money is going to Puerto Rico, instead of into this lady's pocket?" This is the problem that fair trade confronted as it grappled with the question of how to grow: if you want to scale up the system so it is big enough to be really meaningful for a lot of poor Southern farmers, you need to reach a whole lot more consumers. Trust can't flow that far, so you need to provide a guarantee to skeptical consumers that their purchases will make the right kind of difference. Labels are designed to shoulder this enormous burden at the point of purchase.

So, Fairtrade, which is actually a highly complex, product-differentiated and location-specific system for setting and policing labour and environmental standards, for regulating relations and terms of exchange between buyers and sellers, and for certifying producer organizations, is represented to the consumer by a small logo appearing on a product. This logo, and the consumer's belief in its guarantee, is what keeps the system running.

Unfortunately, consumers do not know, and probably cannot be expected to know, much about this underlying system. Identical-looking fair-trade labels actually represent very different labour and environmental standards, depending on the commodity that bears it and where you are buying it. If it is coffee in Canada or the Netherlands, then it means that the farmers who grew the coffee are small-scale and independent, organized through a democratic cooperative structure. If it is coffee in the US or tea in Canada or the UK, then it might have been grown on a plantation and picked by waged workers. Add to this the confusion of consumers who encounter a host of labels in the coffee aisle: Fairtrade, RA certified, Smithsonian bird friendly, organic, Direct Trade or Small Producer.

Then extend this confusion further as you are asked to parse other labels for your lumber, your paper, your seafood, your fruit and vegetables, your sugar, clothing, flowers, chocolate and tea. This is what we mean by asking consumers to look under the hood of the hood. In order genuinely to consume "politically," you are asked to pierce the fog of the commodity – which a label can help you to do. But, as labels begin to compete with one another, consumers are asked to pierce the fog of the label as well. The label itself threatens to become the new fetish – obscuring its origins, what lies behind it, how it is brought into being, what relations it embodies – rather than the commodity itself. This is the price of scaling up beyond networks of trust.

Unfortunately, these labels are credence goods, operating within a competitive market environment, and, given that shoppers have a hard time telling labels apart on the basis of their underlying "ethical content" (the substance and strictness of their standards or their means of verification), this leads to a troubling dynamic. Products made through well-compensated, independent, democratically organized and environmentally friendly forms of labour tend to be higher cost. That is to say, all things being equal, labels with higher labour and environmental standards are going to be stuck to more expensive versions of what otherwise appear to be the same things. If consumers don't know the difference between labels (which they often don't), they'll tend to buy the cheaper item, and, over time, the market will select for the product whose label looks "ethical" but which has the least substance behind it. This is just an extension of Akerlof's famous information problem from chapter 4 (Akerlof, 1970), and it is supported by contemporary research specific to the dynamics of labelling under conditions of imperfect information (Brécard, 2014). There is some evidence that highly engaged consumers work, with some degree of success, to differentiate between labels on the basis of what lies behind them (Lekakis, 2012) and to resist various forms of instrumental cooptation. However, outside of the ranks of the highly committed, it is very doubtful that many people are willing to engage in the amount of work required to peer behind the plethora of labels on the shelves and to treat these labels as substantively different (which they are), rather than as small variations on a shared commitment to "care" (Bratt et al., 2011).

This unwillingness is perfectly understandable, in part because of the constraints on our time, and also because it requires us to cut directly across the grain of a century's worth of effort that went into constructing consumption as a care-free, frivolous realm of fun and hedonistic gratification. As we've seen, most consumption, for most of history, either has not been clearly differentiable from production or has been experienced as a form of work – part of the unpaid household labour, borne largely in Western societies by women. It continues to take on this form, in part. But, since the early days of the high street and the department store, firms and governments have worked to turn consumption into a leisure activity – something you do to relax, to "indulge yourself" and to have fun (figure 7.2). This was a major part of recruiting us into fulfilling the requirement of surplus realization and the spread of shopping-as-entertainment is a major aspect of cultural globalization. For example, since the late 1990s, Dubai has hosted an annual Dubai Shopping Festival, in which "unbeatable retail experiences and deals at your favourite malls and pop-up markets" turn the city into a "must-visit destination" (Dubai Corporation of Tourism and Commercial Marketing, 2019). Shopping appears as a "thing to do" on most cities' tourism websites, where it is depicted

Figure 7.2 Malling is a thing: as malls suffer in many places due to the rise of online shopping, mall culture is thriving in the Philippines.

Source: Business Mirror, 20 May 2019; https://businessmirror.com.ph/2019/05/20/dot-partners-with-sm-for-new-tourism-campaign/.

as wholesome, care-free fun or as a coping mechanism to offset life's other miseries and frustrations.

Political consumerism bursts this carefully constructed bubble. There is little joy in being one small part of an atomized force of consumer enforcers, wondering always in whose blood your next purchase might be soaked. Rather than a pleasure palace, the mall becomes a perplexing house of horrors. Once you start actually doing the work required to consume politically, you become pretty dispirited, pretty fast. Are eggs from "free range" chickens better than eggs from "vegetarian fed" chickens? How many slaves were involved in the production of this shrimp cocktail? Carrying this burden means that even making the most basic of purchases becomes a time-consuming grind. Now your satisfaction in consumption must come from the successful performance of a duty. You have bought the bananas that save the rainforest. You have ordered the coffee that maintains biodiverse shade ecosystems. You lend your weight to sustainable forest management by purchasing the stamped lumber. All of this smacks of drudgery rather than relaxed and carefree leisure. You cannot enjoy the Red Lobster all-you-can-eat shrimp spectacular. It is forbidden to you, and, what's more, you have to do the research to find out why. As such, it is unlikely that consumers themselves – people with jobs, kids, eldercare responsibilities, after-school activities and bills on the kitchen table, not to mention Netflix – are going to embrace yet another dimension of work (especially one so daunting) as part of their shopping.

The other downward pressure on the underlying ethical substance behind labels is the desire or perceived need to engage with big market actors. This is also an important part of scaling up. Reaching more consumers usually means doing so through the large corporations that have access to supermarket shelves or other retail spaces, as well as large current market shares. While these companies initially tried to ignore and then to discredit fair trade as a means of alleviating poverty (Fridell et al., 2008), they have become interested in accessing the growing niche "ethical" consumer market, or at least they don't want to get shut out of it entirely. However, they also don't really want to bind themselves to costly and strict rules about how the coffee or cocoa they buy gets produced, by whom, and at what price they must buy it – all aspects of Fairtrade standards. The way forward has tended to be through negotiation, and the consumer reach of, say, a Starbucks or a Nestlé is a very shiny object indeed to an NGO that wants to move more coffee under the Fairtrade label.

This process of "mainstreaming" Fairtrade (and similar attempts to induce powerful brands and retailers into adopting or selling ethical labels – for example, getting Home Depot to sell FSC-certified lumber or the WWF partnering with the multinational Unilever to create the MSC label) has raised concerns that the standards and terms recognized by consumers as lying behind the label have been or will be watered down or that the "political intensity" of the labels will be weakened (Lekakis, 2012). For example, in a bid to expand the amount of "sustainably sourced" cocoa in chocolate, the UK's Fairtrade Foundation partnered with Mondelez International, which owns Cadbury (Fairtrade Foundation, 2016). The partnership involved Cadbury dropping the Fairtrade label and replacing it with their own "Cocoa Life" ethical label. Observers expressed concern that this might lead to a confusing proliferation of brand-specific ethical labelling (Thomas, 2016), but also that the new scheme contained no minimum price, substituting "loyalty payments," and was 100 percent owned by the company, unlike Fairtrade, which includes growers in its organizational structure (Stock, 2017).

In sum, the attempt to find a convincing, reliable and durable means of helping consumers to see through the "material shell" of the commodity into the relations that bring it into being remains elusive. This is a serious Achilles' heel for a system and a movement that worked so hard, from its origins, to show consumers that commodities that very often looked the same were fundamentally different in the relations that they embody. The ecological shadows that cling to every commodity, as well as the kind of labour that helped bring it into being, vary enormously between objects that appear identical. Fairtrade wanted to present *as* different things that *were* different – coffee grown by brutally exploited workers paid next to nothing by a land-owning boss and coffee grown by a usually poor, small-scale, independent farmer who, through their co-op, gets to decide democratically what to do with any surplus. This is the basis for almost all political consumerism. If labels are increasingly unable to do this – because of information problems, because of competitive market dynamics for labels, and because of the market power of large corporations – then political consumerism as a large-scale phenomenon faces a tough challenge.

The Commodification of Politics?

A second important question with regard to political consumerism is whether it is displacing other forms of politics or changing the way that we understand ourselves in relation to institutions such as markets and governments. That is, does political consumerism involve uncritically adopting the idea that we are primarily consumers rather than citizens and workers?

Despite its long history, political consumerism has risen and fallen in prominence as a tool for social change. But the fact that it has been booming since the 1980s is no coincidence. Just as consumerism itself can be understood partially as a compensatory phenomenon, filling in for other kinds of political gains, satisfactions and sources of meaning in our lives, so political consumerism can be viewed – at least in its current forms – as filling in for other kinds of politics. The relatively recent rise in the success and the scale of ethical consumption has gone hand in hand with the decline of the protective role of the state. In particular, as governments became less willing to regulate businesses in the period of flexible accumulation detailed in chapter 3, stepping back from legislating social and environmental protections and slashing budgets for effective regulation and enforcement, people turned to the market both as a venue for protest and as a means of regulating business. So does political consumerism ask us to take up a neoliberal mantle as "responsibilized" shoppers, bearing a load that properly belongs to regulation by the state?

Consumer choice has long been positioned as an explicit substitute for the political power of individual voting – that is, as a substitute for representative democracy. At times, this kind of narrative was put forward even by proponents of socialist and feminist reform, such as the general secretary of the Women's Co-operative Guild, Margaret Llewelyn Davies, who urged her (largely female) membership to seize their power as shoppers in forwarding workers' aims:

> Her role as the buyer gives the married woman a place of supreme importance, where she can reinforce the claim of her Trade Unionist husband for better industrial conditions by buying goods made only under Trade Union conditions; and where she can take part in forwarding the emancipation of the workers and the peace of the world ... The power of the basket is a greater one than the power of the loom or of the vote. (Quoted in Hilton, 2003: 45, emphasis added)

From the other end of the political spectrum, the Austrian economist Ludwig von Mises was a famous mid-twentieth-century proponent of doing away with mass voting and replacing it with shopping. Rather than seeing consumption as a way of expanding political power for the working classes, as Davies saw it, Mises recognized it as a form of freedom that was more easily and safely containable by elites. Mises believed passionately that universal suffrage was dangerous to a good society because it weakened the prerogatives of property holders, who would likely have their rights undermined by the propertyless mass of voters through the legislated establishment of such things as minimum wages, rights to unionize, or even nationalization of whole industries. Mises held that, regardless of suffrage or voting, "the capitalistic market economy is a democracy, in which every penny constitutes a vote," and in which the rich were elected to their powerful positions by means of a "consumer plebiscite" (quoted in Zevin, 2019: 27). In this view, consumerism and citizenship should – for non-elites – be one and the same. This was contrary to the critiques of consumerism put forward by some of Mises' contemporaries, who considered consumerism and citizenship to be at fundamentally at odds with one another (Kroen, 2004).

In the context of the Cold War, the claim began to emerge that freedom of choice in the market – the freedom to enter into exchange – is not just a freedom in and of itself but is a necessary foundation for political freedom (Friedman, 1962). Should this freedom become regulated or coerced by government, the slide to tyranny would be short and steep. A tight ideological association between freedom and consumerism began to form. Before this, most conceptions of freedom were not about consumer choice but about the extent to which you were dependent on someone else, and the associated extent to which that someone else could arbitrarily control your life. This was the basis of arguments made by abolitionists but also by working-class movements such as the "labour republicans" of the nineteenth-century US, who saw wage labour as a condition of dependency and thus of unfreedom (Gourevitch, 2014). It was only after World War II that consumerism became both an expression of freedom and the primary duty of citizenship (Cohen, 2003). Ideas of market freedom as the form that matters most struggled to gain much traction at the level of government policy through the 1960s and 1970s, but it took firm hold in the 1980s.

While Mises' view that consumer choice was the only form that democracy ought to take hasn't resulted in mass disenfranchisement or the complete restriction of politics to the realm of the market, the conflation of consumerism with democracy has taken fairly deep root in the affluent nations of the Global North. Despite social critiques of consumerism, such as those of Friedan and Marcuse, appearing in the post-war period, it has become almost common sense to think that consumer choice is a key element of democracy. Choice is understood as a means through which we "govern." Political consumerism makes use of this common sense by trying to establish a direct governance relationship between consumers and corporations without relying on the mediating authority of the state. It also responds to the perceived limits of states in a world of globalized production, in which one's consumption-related complicity in human rights violations, exploitation and despoliation spills over the boundaries of nation-states. It asks consumers in Paris to recognize and to regulate, in a way that the French government cannot, the actions of a corporation in Senegal or Vietnam.

However, while nervousness about people embracing a purely market-based political subjectivity abounds, there does not appear to be much convincing evidence that political consumerism is supplanting other vehicles of politics, such as voting or participating in protests and demonstrations. It may, in fact, be a "gateway" form of politics that opens people to more collective action, or it may be seen by participants as one among a bundle of important tactics that all need to be utilized to achieve social goals (for a review of this evidence in Canada and Europe, and for its own study of the US, see Willets and Schor, 2012; see also Heldman, 2017: 208).

Conclusion

The political economy of consumption alerts us to the dangers of a politics based on "individual choice" and "ethical consumerism" which absolves government of its regulatory role and charges consumers with social and environmental oversight for which they are ill equipped, even given technologies and bureaucracies intended to aid that function. It points us in the direction of understanding consumption as a terrain of struggle and as a set of normatively, institutionally and materially structured practices. Those practices do not take place under conditions that are freely chosen, and there are enormous implications to engaging in voluntarist, uncoordinated "defections" from these – both for the individual and for the dominant economic system. That is in no way a claim intended to elicit shrugs and a hopeless return to hedonistic consumption. While the difficulties and pitfalls we have discussed are daunting indeed, overcoming them is a challenge worth taking on. This is because initiatives based on political consumerism, such as Fairtrade or the FSC, have managed to do two things – if incompletely and in a compromised way – that are politically important and rare. The first of these is to begin training consumers to think about the social and environmental implications of their consumption – to refuse to see commodities as they appear – and to view their day-to-day consumption practices as embedded in systems that precede them, but in whose reproduction they participate. Much of what we have discussed up to this point indicates how difficult it is to do anything about this in practice. A great deal is stacked against us – infrastructures, invisible or hidden side-effects, social expectations and norms, histories of class- and gender-based struggle, even an overarching cultural orientation to meaning and freedom. But the "recruitment" process relies to a significant extent on consumers being open to interpretations of the reality of commodities generated by the companies that produce and retail them. Does a running shoe – which on the surface is just a more or less functional assemblage of rubber and textiles – actually connect me to performance, resolve, determination, fashion, celebrity or athleticism, as the marketers would have it? Or does it connect me to the poverty of the seamstress and the toxicity of petrochemical refining?

The second thing is that, while the rise of this individual, ethical regulatory consumerism is indeed neoliberal, the bureaucracies on which consumers rely – the certifying agencies that generate the credible promise of ethical production – actually do require some access to decision-making power over the process of production. Some of the more activist-led labelling and certification schemes, such as the FSC and the Fairtrade labelling organization, have thus managed something that is crucial. They have, where labour unions and states have struggled to do so, cracked open the largely sealed world in which decisions about what to produce and how to produce it are taken. They have forced some very small segments of the corporate world to reckon with criteria beyond pure profit in order to gain access to a valuable splinter of the consumer market. They dictate (in the stronger cases – in the weaker ones, they negotiate) how much will be cut, how much harvested, using what techniques, under what conditions and relations of labour, paying what wages, and with what effects on nature. Operating in the market, labels with strict standards are always likely to be undercut by lookalikes and cheap "ethical" knock-offs. Their survival depends on consumers actually accepting the duty-bound and depressing version of consumption rather than the fun-filled one. But if Daniel Miller's (1998) research on consumption as an act of care extended to family members is right, we can ask whether that care can be extended beyond the family, in solidarity with producers. If consumers can reconceptualize consumption as an act that carries extended responsibility, and as they are frustrated by the market-imposed limits of their capacity to discharge that responsibility adequately, they may yet realize that this duty of care is best undertaken by publicly controlled organizations with enforcement capabilities that transcend those granted by the pocketbook (that is, they acknowledge the possibility and necessity of forcing the state to act in the public interest). In this way, political consumerism might provide a wedge for making democratic decisions about what we make and how – which is the only way to arrive at just and sustainable systems of provisioning.

References

Ackerman, F. (1997) Consumed in Theory: Alternative Perspectives on the Economics of Consumption, *Journal of Economic Issues*, 31/3: 651–64.

Adorno, T. W., and Horkheimer, M. (1997) *Dialectic of Enlightenment*. New York: Verso.

Aglietta, M. (1979) *A Theory of Capitalist Regulation: The US Experience*. London: Verso.

Akerlof, G. A. (1970) The Market for "Lemons": Quality Uncertainty and the Market Mechanism, *Quarterly Journal of Economics*, 84/3: 488–500.

Akerlof, G., and Shiller, R. (2015) *Phishing for Phools: The Economics of Manipulation and Deception*. Princeton, NJ: Princeton University Press.

Allegretto, S. (2011) *The State of Working America's Wealth 2011*, Briefing Paper no. 292. Washington, DC: Economic Policy Institute.

Alphabet (2019) *Annual Report 2019*. Mountain View, CA: Alphabet.

Alsheh, Y. (2019) Sanctions against South Africa: Myths, Debates, and Consequences, in *Boycotts Past and Present: From the American Revolution to the Campaign to Boycott Israel*. New York: Palgrave Macmillan, pp. 175–96.

Arnould, E. J. (2011) Consumer Culture in Africa, in D. Southerton (ed.), *Encyclopedia of Consumer Culture*. Thousand Oaks, CA: Sage, pp. 245–7.

Avins, J. (2017) A History of Aspiration, from Socrates' "Luxurious State" to Instagram Envy, *Quartzy*, 8 November.

Baragar, F., and Chernomas, R. (2012) Profits from Production and Profits from Exchange: Financialization, Household

Debt and Profiability in 21st-Century Capitalism, *Science & Society*, 76/3: 319–39.

Baran, P., and Sweezy, P. (1966) *Monopoly Capital*. New York: Monthly Review Press.

Baudrillard, J. ([1969] 1981) *For a Critique of the Political Economy of the Sign*. St Louis: Telos Press.

Bauer, A. (2001) *Goods, Power, History*. Cambridge: Cambridge University Press.

Bauman, Z. (2008) Industrialism, Consumerism, and Power, in D. Clark, M. Doel and K. Housiaux (eds), *The Consumption Reader*. New York: Routledge, pp. 54–60.

Becker, G. S. (1976) *The Economic Approach to Human Behavior*. Chicago: University of Chicago Press.

Becker, U. J., Becker, T., and Gerlach, J. (2012) *The True Costs of Automobility: External Costs of Cars: Overview on existing estimates in EU-27*. Dresden: Technische Universität Dresden.

Bennett, J. N. (2019) *Fast Cash and Payday Loans*, https://research.stlouisfed.org/publications/page1-econ/2019/04/10/fast-cash-and-payday-loans.

Bentham, J. (1780) *An Introduction to the Principles of Morals and Legislation*. London: T. Payne & Son.

Berg, M. (2012) Luxury, the Luxury Trades, and the Roots of Industrial Growth: A Global Perspective, in F. Trentmann (ed.), *The Oxford Handbook of the History of Consumption*. New York: Oxford University Press, pp. 173–91.

Bernstein, M. (2009) *Propaganda and Prejudice Distort the Health Reform Debate*, www.healthaffairs.org/do/10.1377/hblog20090422.000947/full/.

Bes-Rastrollo, M., Schulze, M., Ruiz-Canela, M., and Martinez-Gonzalez, M. (2013) Financial Conflicts of Interest and Reporting Bias regarding the Association between Sugar-Sweetened Beverages and Weight Gain: A Systematic Review of Systematic Reviews, *PLOS Medicine*, 10/12: e1001578.

Bird, M. M., and Robinson, J. W. (1972) The Effectiveness of the Union Label and "Buy Union" Campaigns, *ILR Review*, 25/4: 512–23.

Biswas, D. (2009) The Effects of Option Framing on Consumer Choices: Making Decisions in Rational versus Experiential

Processing Modes, *Journal of Consumer Behaviour*, 8/5: 284–99.

Bonneuil, C., and Fressoz, J. (2015) *The Shock of the Anthropocene*. London: Verso.

Bourdieu, P. (1984) *Distinction*. Abingdon: Routledge.

Bourdieu, P. ([1988] 2016) *The Social Structures of the Economy*. Cambridge: Polity.

Bowen, S., Brenton, J., and Sinikka, E. (2019) *Pressure Cooker: Why Home Cooking Won't Solve Our Problems, and What We Can Do about It*. New York: Oxford University Press.

Bowles, S., Gordon, D. M., and Weisskopf, T. E. (1986) Power and Profits: The Social Structure of Accumulation and the Profitability of the Postwar U.S. Economy, *Review of Radical Political Economics*, 18/1–2: 132–67.

Bratt, C., et al. (2011) Assessment of Eco-Labelling Criteria Development from a Strategic Sustainability Perspective, *Journal of Cleaner Production*, 19: 1631–8.

Brécard, D. (2014) Consumer Confusion over the Profusion of Eco-Labels: Lessons from a Double-Differentiation Model, *Resource and Energy Economics*, 37: 64–84.

Bronfenbrenner, K. (2009) *No Holds Barred: The Intensification of Employer Opposition to Organizing*. Washington, DC: Economic Policy Institute.

Brooks, A. (2015) *Clothing Poverty: The Hidden World of Fast Fashion and Second-Hand Clothes*. London: Zed Books.

Cahalan, M., and Perna, L. (2015) *Indicators of Higher Education Equity in the US*. Washington, DC: Pell Institute.

Campbell, C. ([1987] 2018) *The Romantic Ethic and the Spirit of Modern Consumerism*. New extended edn, London: Palgrave Macmillan.

Caplovitz, D. (1966) *The Mass Consumption Society*, George Katona, *American Journal of Sociology*, 72/1: 117–18 [book review].

Carrington, D. (2017) Plastic Fibres Found in Tap Water around the World, Study Reveals, *The Guardian*, 6 September.

Cayla, J., and Peñaloza, L. (2011) Mapping the Future of Consumers, in D. Zwick and J. Cayla (eds), *Inside*

Marketing: Practices, Ideologies, Devices. Oxford: Oxford University Press, pp. 320–42.

Chan, T., and Goldthorpe, J. (2007) Social Stratification and Cultural Consumption: Music in England, *European Sociological Review*, 23: 1–19.

Chapagain, A., Hoekstra, A., Savenige, H., and Gautam, R. (2006) The Water Footprint of Cotton Consumption: An Assessment of the Impact of Worldwide Consumption of Cotton Products on the Water Resources in the Cotton Producing Countries, *Ecological Economics*, 60: 186–203.

Clark, A., Frijters, P., and Shields, M. (2008) Relative Income, Happiness, and Utility: An Explanation for the Easterlin Paradox and Other Puzzles, *Journal of Economic Literature*, 46/1: 95–144.

Clarke, D., Doel, M., and Housiaux, K. (2003) Introduction, in D. Clarke, M. Doel and K. Housiaux (eds), *The Consumption Reader*. New York: Routledge, pp. 27–31.

Clunas, C. (2012) Things in Between: Splendour and Excess in Ming China, in F. Trentmann (ed.), *The Oxford Handbook of the History of Consumption*. New York: Oxford University Press, pp. 47–63.

Coase, R. ([1960] 2013) The Problem of Social Cost, *Journal of Law and Economics*, 56/4: 837–77.

Cohen, L. (2003) *A Consumers' Republic: The Politics of Mass Consumption in Postwar America*. New York: Alfred A. Knopf.

Cohen, L. (2004) A Consumers' Republic: The Politics of Mass Consumption in Postwar America, *Journal of Consumer Research*, 31: 236–9.

Cole, N. L., and Crossley, A. D. (2009) On Feminism in the Age of Consumption, *Consumers, Commodities & Consumption*, 11/1.

Crary, J. (2013) *24/7 Late Capitalism and the Ends of Sleep*. New York: Verso.

Cross, G. (2000) *An All-Consuming Century: Why Commercialism Won in Modern America*. New York: Columbia University Press.

Currid-Halkett, E. (2017) *The Sum of Small Things: A Theory of the Aspirational Class*. Princeton, NJ: Princeton University Press.

Dammert, A. C., and Mohan, S. (2015) A Survey of the

Economics of Fair Trade, *Journal of Economic Surveys*, 29/5: 855–68.

Darby, M. R., and Karni, E. (1973) Free Competition and the Optimal Amount of Fraud, *Journal of Law and Economics*, 16/1: 67–88.

Dauvergne, P. (2010) *The Shadows of Consumption: Consequences for the Global Environment*. Cambridge, MA: MIT Press.

Davidson, P. (2015) *Post Keynesian Theory and Policy: A Realistic Analysis of the Market Oriented Capitalist Economy*. Cheltenham: Edward Elgar.

Dawson, M. (2003) *The Consumer Trap: Big Business Marketing in American Life*. Urbana: University of Illinois Press.

De Luce, I. (2019) 10 Companies That Spent More Than $1 Billion in Ads so You'd Buy Their Products, www.businessinsider.com/10-biggest-advertising-spenders-in-the-us-2015-7.

Deaton, A. (2008) Income, Health, and Well-Being around the World: Evidence from the Gallup World Poll, *Journal of Economic Perspective*, 22/2: 53–72.

Delaney, B. (2017) The Yoga Industry is Booming – but Does it Make You a Better Person?, *The Guardian*, 17 September.

Deutsch, N., and Theodorou, E. (2010) Aspiring, Consuming, Becoming: Youth Identity in a Culture of Consumption, *Youth & Society*, 42/2: 229–54.

Dholakia, N., and Fuat Firat, A. (1998) *Consuming People: From Political Economy to Theaters of Consumption*. London: Routledge.

Doucouliagos, C. (1994) A Note on the Evolution of Homo Economicus, *Journal of Economic Issues*, 28/3: 877–83.

Douglas, M., and Isherwood, B. (1979) *The World of Goods: Toward an Anthropology of Consumption*. London: Routledge.

Dubai Corporation of Tourism and Commercial Marketing (2019) Dubai Shopping Festival 2020, www.visitdubai.com/en/dsf.

Duesenberry, J. (1949) *Income, Saving, and the Theory of Consumer Behavior*. Cambridge, MA: Harvard University Press.

Durning, A. (1992) *How Much Is Enough? The Consumer Society and the Future of the Earth.* New York: W. W. Norton.

Easterlin, R. (1974) Does Economic Growth Improve the Human Lot?, in *Nations and Households in Economic Growth: Essays in Honour of Moses Abramovitz.* New York: Academic Press, pp. 89–126.

Easterlin, R. (1995) Will Raising the Incomes of All Increase the Happiness of All?, *Journal of Economic Behavior and Organization*, 27/1: 35–48.

Ehrenreich, J. (2016) *Third Wave Capitalism: How Money, Power, and the Pursuit of Self-Interest Have Imperiled the American Dream.* Ithaca, NY: ILR Press.

Engels, F. (1850) *The Conditions of the Working Class in England in 1844.* London: Allen & Unwin.

England, P. (1993) The Separative Self: Androcentric Bias in Neoclassical Assumptions, in M. A. Ferber and J. A. Nelson (eds), *Beyond Economic Man: Feminist Theory and Economics.* Chicago: University of Chicago Press, pp. 37–53.

Fairtrade Federation (n.d.) A Brief History of Fair Trade, www.fairtradefederation.org/resources/a-brief-history-of-fair-trade/.

Fairtrade Foundation (2016) *Cocoa Life Sustainability Programme Expands to Cover Cadbury Chocolate through New Partnership with Fairtrade*, www.fairtrade.org.uk/en/media-centre/news/november-2016/cocoa-life-and-fairtrade-partnership.

Fairtrade International (2019) *Monitoring the Scope and Benefits of Fairtrade: Overall.* Bonn: Fairtrade International.

Federici, S. (2012) *Revolution at Point Zero: Housework, Reproduction, and Feminist Struggle.* Oakland, CA: PM Press.

Feldman, D. (2019) Boycotts: From the American Revolution to BDS, in D. Feldman (ed.), *Boycotts Past and Present: From the American Revolution to the Campaign to Boycott Israel.* New York: Palgrave Macmillan, pp. 1–20.

Fine, B. (2002) *The World of Consumption: The Material and the Cultural.* New York: Routledge.

Fishman, C. (2006) *The Wal-Mart Effect: How the World's*

Most Powerful Company Really Works – and How it's Transforming the American Economy. New York: Penguin Books.

Fiske, J. (1989) *Understanding Popular Culture*. Boston: Unwin Hyman.

Fiske, J. (1992) Cultural Studies and the Culture of Everyday Life, in L. Grossman, C. Nelson and P. A. Treichler (eds), *Cultural Studies*. London: Routledge, pp. 154–73.

Fiske, J. (2011) *Reading the Popular*. 2nd edn, London: Routledge.

Fones-Wolf, E. (1994) *Selling Free Enterprise: The Business Assault on Labor and Liberalism, 1945–60*. Urbana: University of Illinois Press.

Fort, R., and Ruben, R. (2009) The impact of Fair Trade Certification on Coffee Producers in Peru, in R. Ruben (ed.), *The Impact of Fair Trade*. Wageningen: Wageningen Academic, pp. 75–98.

Frank, R. (1985) *Choosing the Right Pond: Human Behavior and the Quest for Status*. New York: Oxford University Press.

Frank, R. (1999) *Luxury Fever: Money and Happiness in an Era of Excess*. Princeton, NJ: Princeton University Press.

Frank, R. (2007) *Richistan: A Journey through the American Wealth Boom and the Lives of the New Rich*. New York: Crown.

Frank, R. (2013) *Falling Behind: How Rising Inequality Harms the Middle Class*. Oakland: University of California Press.

Frank, T. (1997) Alternative to What?, in T. Frank and M. Weiland (eds), *Commodify Your Dissent: Salvos from the Baffler*. New York: W. W. Norton.

Fraser, S. (2015) *The Age of Acquiescence: The Life and Death of American Resistance to Organized Wealth and Power*. New York: Little, Brown.

Frederick, S., Loewenstein, G., and O'Donoghue, T. (2002) Time Discounting and Time Preference: A Critical Review, *Journal of Economic Literature*, 40/2: 351–401.

Fridell, M., Hudson, I., and Hudson, M. (2008) With Friends Like These …: The Corporate Response to Fair Trade Coffee, *Review of Radical Political Economics*, 40/1: 8–34.

Friedan, B. (1963) *The Feminine Mystique*. New York: Dell.

Friedman, L. (2014) John Oliver Takes on the Sugar Industry in His Latest Hilarious Rant, *Business Insider*, 27 October.

Friedman, M. (1953) The Methodology of Positive Economics, in M. Friedman (ed.), *Essays in Positive Economics*. Chicago: University of Chicago Press, pp. 3–43.

Friedman, M. (1962) *Capitalism and Freedom*. Chicago: University of Chicago Press.

Fromm, J. (2018) How Much Financial Influence Does Gen Z Have?, *Forbes*, 10 January.

Galbraith, J. (1958) *The Affluent Society*. Boston: Houghton Mifflin.

George, R. (2013) *Ninety Percent of Everything: Inside Shipping, the Invisible Industry that Puts Clothes on Your Back, Gas in Your Car, and Food on Your Plate*. New York: Metropolitan Books.

Gibbs, S. (2018) Apple and Samsung Fined for Deliberately Slowing Down Phones, *The Guardian*, 24 October.

Glickman, L. (2004) "Buy for the Sake of the Slave": Abolitionism and the Origins of American Consumer Activism, *American Quarterly*, 56/4: 889–912.

Glickman, L. B. (2009) *Buying Power: A History of Consumer Activism in America*. Chicago: University of Chicago Press.

Global Footprint Network (2019) *Global Footprint Network Open Data Platform*, http://data.footprintnetwork.org/?_ga=2.202050770.2121636358.1573331083-929762351.1573331083#/.

Goleman, G., and Norris, G. (2009) Op Chart: How Green is my Bottle?, *New York Times*, 19 April.

Gourevitch, A. (2014) *From Slavery to the Cooperative Commonwealth: Labor and Republican Liberty in the Nineteenth Century*. New York: Cambridge University Press.

Gourevitch, A. (2015) Police Work: The Centrality of Labor Repression in American Political History, *Perspectives on Politics*, 13/3: 762–73.

Gramsci, A. (1978) *Selections from the Prison Notebooks*. New York: International.

Grynbaum, M. M., and Maheshwari, S. (2017) As Anger at O'Reilly Builds, Activists Use Social Media to Prod Advertisers, *New York Times*, 6 April.

Guard, J. (2019) *Radical Housewives: Price Wars and Food Politics in Mid-Twentieth Century Canada.* Toronto: University of Toronto Press.

Guckian, M. L., Chapman, D. A., Lickel, B., and Markowitz, E. M. (2017) "A Few Bad Apples" or "Rotten to the Core": Perceptions of Corporate Culture Drive Brand Engagement after Corporate Scandal, *Journal of Consumer Behaviour*, 17/1: 29–41.

Halnon, K. B. (2005) Alienation Incorporated: "F*** the Mainstream Music" in the Mainstream, *Current Sociology*, 53/3: 441–64.

Harvey, D. (1990) *The Condition of Postmodernity.* Oxford: Wiley-Blackwell.

Haug, W. (1986) *Critique of Commodity Aesthetics: Appearance, Sexuality, and Advertising in Capitalist Society.* Cambridge: Polity.

Haupt, H.-G. (2012) Small Shops and Department Stores, in F. Trentmann (ed.), *The Oxford Handbook of the History of Consumption.* New York: Oxford University Press, pp. 267–88.

Hebidge, R. (1979) *Subculture: The Meaning of Style.* London: Routledge.

Hebidge, R. (1988) *Hiding in the Light: On Images and Things.* London: Routledge.

Heldman, C. (2017) *Protest Politics in the Marketplace: Consumer Activism in the Corporate Age.* Ithaca, NY: Cornell University Press.

Helliwell, J., and Huang, H. (2008) How's Your Government? International Evidence Linking Good Government and Well-Being, *British Journal of Political Science*, 38/4: 595–619.

Helliwell, J., and Putnam, R. (2004) The Social Context of Well-Being, *Philosophical Transactions of the Royal Society of London*, 339/1449: 1445–56.

Hemenway, D., et al. (1990) Physicians' Responses to Financial Incentives: Evidence from a For-Profit Ambulatory Care Center, *New England Journal of Medicine*, 322/15: 1059–63.

Hillman, A., Pauly, M., and Kerstein, J. (1989) How Do Financial Incentives Affect Physicians' Clinical Decisions and the Financial Performance of Health Maintenance

Organizations?, *New England Journal of Medicine*, 321/2: 86–92.

Hilton, M. (2003) *Consumerism in Twentieth-Century Britain: The Search for a Historical Movement*. Cambridge: Cambridge University Press.

Hobsbawm, E. (1964) *Labouring Men*. New York: Basic Books.

Hobsbawm, E. (1975) *The Age of Capital 1848–1875*. London: Weidenfeld & Nicolson.

Holt, D., and Cameron, D. (2010) *Cultural Strategy: Using Innovative Ideologies to Build Breakthrough Brands*. Oxford: Oxford University Press.

Hosseini, H. (2017) George Katona's Contributions to the Start of Behavioral Economics, in R. Frantz et al. (eds), *Routledge Handbook of Behavioral Economics*. New York: Routledge.

Hudson, I. (2009) From Deregulation to Crisis, in J. Guard and W. Antony (eds), *Bankruptcies and Bailouts*. Winnipeg: Fernwood.

Hudson, I., and Hudson, M. (2003) Removing the Veil: Commodity Fetishism, Fair Trade, and the Environment, *Organization and Environment*, 16/4: 413–40.

Hudson, M., Hudson, I., and Fridell, M. (2013) *Fair Trade, Sustainability, and Social Change*. New York: Palgrave Macmillan.

Huff, Q. B. (2011) Walk This Way: The Commodification of Hip-Hop, www.popmatters.com/135317-walk-this-way-the-commodification-of-hip-hop-2496094049.html?rebelltitem=3#rebelltitem3.

Hunt, A. (2003) Societies of Consumers and Consumer Societies, in D. Clarke, M. Doel and K. Housiaux (eds), *The Consumption Reader*. New York: Routledge, pp. 62–8.

Hunt, E. (1979) *History of Economic Thought: A Critical Perspective*. Belmont, CA: Wadsworth.

Inani, R. (2020) Is the Indian Economy Headed for a Middle-Income Trap?, https://qz.com/india/1783927/indias-slowing-gdp-could-lead-to-a-middle-income-trap/.

Inglehart, R. (2007) Postmaterialist Values and the Shift from Survival to Self-Expression Values, in R. Dalton and H.-D.

Klingemann (eds), *The Oxford Handbook of Political Behavior.* Oxford: Oxford University Press, pp. 223–39.

International Council on Clean Transportation (2019) *European Vehicle Market Statistics: Pocketbook 2018/19.* Berlin: ICCT.

International Maritime Organization (2014) *Third IMO GHG Study.* London: International Maritime Organization.

IPCC (2018) *Global Warming of 1.5°C: An IPCC Special Report on the Impacts of Global Warming of 1.5°C above Pre-Industrial Levels and Related Global Greenhouse Gas Emission Pathways, in the Context of Strengthening the Global Response to the Threat of Climate Change.* Geneva: IPCC.

Jackson, T. (2009) *Prosperity without Growth.* London: Earthscan.

Jaffee, D. (2007) *Brewing Justice: Fair Trade Coffee, Sustainability, and Survival.* Berkeley: University of California Press.

Jena, P. R., and Grote, U. (2017) Fairtrade Certification and Livelihood Impacts on Small-Scale Coffee Producers in a Tribal Community of India, *Applied Economic Perspectives and Policy*, 39/1: 87–110.

Jessop, B. (1997) Survey Article: The Regulation Approach, *Journal of Political Philosophy*, 5/3: 287–326.

Jevons, W. ([1871] 1957) *The Theory of Political Economy.* 5th edn, New York: Sentry Press.

Jhally, S. (1987) *The Codes of Advertising: Fetishism and the Political Economy of Meaning in the Consumer Society.* New York: Routledge.

Jones, J. (2007) *When Ads Work: New Proof that Advertising Triggers Sales.* New York: M. E. Sharpe.

Jonsson, P. O. (1994) Social Influence and Individual Preferences: On Schumpeter's Theory of Consumer Choice, *Review of Social Economy*, 52/4: 301–14.

Jowitt, J. (2010) World's Top Firms Cause $2.2tn of Environmental Damage, Report Estimates, *The Guardian*, 18 February.

Kahneman, D. (2003) Maps of Bounded Rationality: Psychology for Behavioral Economics, *American Economic Review*, 93/5: 1449–75.

Kahneman, D., and Tversky, A. (1979) Prospect Theory:

An Analysis of Decision under Risk, *Econometrica*, 47/2: 263–92.

Kahr, A., Nyffenegger, B., Krohmer, H., and Hoyer, W. D. (2016) When Hostile Consumers Wreak Havoc on Your Brand: The Phenomenon of Consumer Brand Sabotage, *Journal of Marketing*, 80: 25–41.

Kalecki, M. (1943) Political Aspects of Full Employment, *Political Quarterly*, 14/4: 322–30.

Kalecki, M. (1971) *Selected Essays on the Dynamics of the Capitalist Economy 1933–1970*. Cambridge: Cambridge University Press.

Kantwill, P. E., and Peterson, C. L. (2019) American Usury Law and the Military Lending Act, *Loyola Consumer Law Review*, 31/3: 498–545.

Katona, G. (1960) *The Powerful Consumer: Psychological Studies of the American Economy*. New York: McGraw-Hill.

Katona, G. (1964) *The Mass Consumption Society*. New York: McGraw-Hill.

Keynes, J. (1936) *The General Theory of Employment, Interest and Money*. London: Macmillan.

Khan, S., and Malik, A. (2013) Environmental and Health Effects of Textile Industry Wastewater, in A. Malik, E. Grohmann and R. Akhtar (eds), *Environmental Deterioration and Human Health*. Dordrecht: Springer, pp. 55–71.

Kimmerer, R. W. (2013) *Braiding Sweetgrass*. Minneapolis: Milkweed Editions.

King, J. (2008) Post Keynesian Economics, in S. Durlauf and L. Blume (eds), *The New Palgrave Dictionary of Economics*. Basingstoke: Palgrave Macmillan.

Klein, N. (2000) *No Logo: Taking Aim at the Brand Bullies*. Toronto: Random House.

Kotz, D. (2015) *The Rise and Fall of Neoliberal Capitalism*. Cambridge, MA: Harvard University Press.

Kroen, S. (2004) A Political History of the Consumer, *Historical Journal*, 47/3: 709–36.

Kyrk, H. ([1923] 2010) The Nature and Scope of a Study of Consumption, in D. K. Barker and E. Kuiper (eds), *Feminist Economics*. New York: Routledge, pp. 168–82.

Lancaster, K. J. (1966) A New Approach to Consumer Theory, *Journal of Political Economy*, 74/2: 132–57.

Lavoie, M. (1994) A Post Keynesian Approach to Consumer Choice, *Journal of Post Keynesian Economics*, 16/4: 539–62.

Lavoie, M. (2019) Modern Monetary Theory and Post-Keynesian Economics, *Real-World Economics Review*, no. 89: 97–108.

Lawrence, E., Woodward, C., Meyer, Z., and Tanner, K. (2018) Death on Foot: Pedestrian Fatalities Skyrocket in U.S., *Detroit Free Press*, 8 May.

Lekakis, E. J. (2012) Will the Fair Trade Revolution Be Marketised? Commodification, Decommodification and the Political Intensity of Consumer Politics, *Culture and Organization*, 18/5: 345–58.

Lizardo, O., and Skiles, S. (2015) After Omnivorousness: Is Bourdieu Still Relevant?, in L. Hanquinet and M. Savage (eds), *Routledge International Handbook of the Sociology of Art and Culture*. New York: Routledge, pp. 90–103.

Lorenz, T. (2019) Emma Chamberlain is the Most Important YouTuber Today, www.theatlantic.com/technology/archive/2019/07/emma-chamberlain-and-rise-relatable-influencer/593230/.

Luxton, M. (2017) Rethinking Social Reproduction through the Multi-Dimensional Woman, in T. Maley (ed.), *One-Dimensional Man 50 Years On: The Struggle Continues*. Halifax: Fernwood Press.

Magsaysay, M. (2018) How Cardi B Makes Fashion Moves, www.businessoffashion.com/articles/intelligence/how-cardi-b-makes-fashion-moves.

Mandeville, B. (1732) *The Fable of the Bees or Private Vices, Publick Benefits*. Oxford: Clarendon Press.

Manning, R. (2000) *Credit Card Nation: The Consequences of America's Addiction to Credit*. New York: Basic Books.

Manno, J. (2002) Commoditization, in T. Princen, M. Maniates and K. Conca (eds), *Confronting Consumption*. Cambridge, MA: MIT Press.

Marçal, K. (2016) *Who Cooked Adam Smith's Dinner? A Story About Women and Economics*. New York: Pegasus Books.

Marcuse, H. ([1964] 1991) *One-Dimensional Man: Studies*

in the Ideology of Advanced Industrial Society. London: Routledge.

Margairaz, D. (2012) City and Country: Home, Possessions, and Diet, Western Europe 1600–1800, in F. Trentmann (ed.), *The Oxford Handbook of the History of Consumption*. New York: Oxford University Press, pp. 192–210.

Marshall, A. (1890) *Principles of Economics*. London: Macmillan.

Martin, F., Lewis, T., and Sinclair, J. (2013) Lifestyle Media and Social Transformation in Asia, *Media International Australia*, no. 147: 51–61.

Marx, K. ([1867] 1976) *Capital: A Critique of Political Economy*. Chicago: Charles H. Kerr.

Marx, K. (1977) *Economic and Philosophic Manuscripts of 1844*. Moscow: Progress.

Mathur, N. (2010) Shopping Malls, Credit Cards, and Global Brands: Consumer Culture and Lifestyle of India's New Middle Class, *South Asia Research*, 30/3: 211–31.

Maughan, T.(2015) The Dystopian Lake Filled by the World's Tech Lust, *BBC Future*, 2 April.

McCabe, I. (2015) *A History of Global Consumption: 1500–1800*. Abingdon: Routledge.

McCracken, G. (1987) The History of Consumption: A Literature Review and Consumer Guide, *Journal of Consumption Policy*, 10/2: 139–66.

McCracken, G. (1988) *Culture and Consumption: New Approaches to the Symbolic Character of Consumer Goods and Activities*. Bloomington: Indiana University Press.

McDonald, M. C. (2012) Transatlantic Consumption, in F. Trentmann (ed.), *The Oxford Handbook of the History of Consumption*. Oxford: Oxford University Press, pp. 111–26.

McKendrick, N., Brewer, J., and Plumb, J. (1982) *The Birth of a Consumer Society: The Commercialization of Eighteenth-Century England*. Bloomington: Indiana University Press.

McRobbie, A. (1997) Bridging the Gap: Feminism, Fashion, and Consumption, *Feminist Review*, 55: 73–89.

McRobbie, A. (2015) Notes on the Perfect: Competitive

Femininity in Neoliberal Times, *Australian Feminist Studies*, 30/83: 3–20.

Meadows, D., Meadows, D., Randers, J., Behrens III, W. W. (1972) *The Limits to Growth*. New York: Universe Books.

Menger, C., ([1871] 2007) *Principles of Economics*. Auburn, AL: Ludwig von Mises Institute.

Milestone, K., and Meyer, A. (2012) *Gender and Popular Culture*. Cambridge: Polity.

Mill, J. S. (1885) *Principles of Political Economy*. New York: D. Appleton.

Mill, J. S. (1909) *Principles of Political Economy, with Some of their Applications to Social Philosophy*. 7th edn, London: Longmans, Green.

Miller, D. (1998) *A Theory of Shopping*. Ithaca, NY: Cornell University Press.

Mishel, L. (2012) CEO Pay 231 Times Greater than the Average Worker, www.epi.org/publication/ceo-pay-231-times-greater-average-worker/.

Mukerji, C. (1983) *From Graven Images: Patterns in Modern Materialism*. New York: Columbia University Press.

Muller, D. (2019) Light Trucks Take a Record 69% of U.S. Market, www.autonews.com/sales/light-trucks-take-record-69-us-market.

Nabi, N., O'Cass, A., and Siahtiri, V. (2019) Status Consumption in Newly Emerging Countries: The Influence of Personality Traits and the Mediating Role of Motivation to Consume Conspicuously, *Journal of Retailing and Consumer Services*, 46: 173–8.

Nelson, J. (1996) *Feminism, Objectivity, and Economics*. New York: Routledge.

Nelson, P. (1970) Information and Consumer Behavior, *Journal of Political Economy*, 78/2: 311–29.

Nelson, P. (1974) Advertising as Information, *Journal of Political Economy*, 82/4: 729–54.

Nersisyan, Y., and Wray, L. (2019) *How to Pay for the Green New Deal*, Working Paper no. 931. Annandale-on-Hudson, NY: Levy Economics Institute.

Nestle, M. (2013) *Food Politics: How the Food Industry Influences Nutrition and Health*. 10th edn, Berkeley: University of California Press.

Neve, M. (2009) Advertising and the Middle-Class Female

Consumer in Munich, *Business and Economic History Online*, 7: 1–9.

Neve, M. (2010) *Sold! Advertising and the Bourgeois Female Consumer in Munich 1900–1914*. Stuttgart: Franz Steiner.

Newhouse, J. (1993) *Free For All? Lessons from the Rand Health Insurance Experiment*. Cambridge, MA: Harvard University Press.

Nunn, N. (2008) The Long Term Effects of Africa's Slave Trades, *Quarterly Journal of Economics*, 123/1: 139–76.

Ocasio-Cortez, A. (2019) *H.Res.109 – Recognizing the Duty of the Federal Government to Create a Green New Deal*, www.congress.gov/bill/116th-congress/house-resolution/109/text.

O'Connor, J. (1988) Capitalism, Nature, Socialism: A Theoretical Introduction, *Capitalism, Nature, Socialism*, 1/1: 11–38.

O'Donoghue, T., and Rabin, M. (1999) Doing it Now or Later, *American Economic Review*, 89/1: 103–24.

OECD (2013) *Material Resources, Productivity, and the Environment: Key Findings*. Paris: OECD.

O'Hara, S. (1999) Economics, Ecology, and Quality of Life: Who Evaluates?, *Feminist Economics*, 5/2: 83–9.

Pandya, S. S., and Venkatesan, R. (2016) French Roast: Consumer Response to International Conflict: Evidence from Supermarket Scanner Data, *Review of Economics and Statistics*, 98/1: 42–56.

Pasinetti, L. (1981) *Structural Change and Economic Growth*. Cambridge: Cambridge University Press.

Passell, P., Roberts, M., and Ross, L. (1972) The Limits to Growth, *New York Times*, 2 April, Section BR, p. 1 [book review].

Paterson, M. (2017) *Consumption and Everyday Life*. New York: Routledge.

Pellow, D. N. (2018) *What is Critical Environmental Justice?* Cambridge: Polity.

Pennell, S. (2012) Material Culture in Seventeenth-Century "Britain": The Matter of Domestic Consumption, in F. Trentmann (ed.), *The Oxford Handbook of the History of Consumption* (Oxford: Oxford University Press, 2012).

Perry, V. G. (2019) A Loan at Last? Race and Racism in Mortgage Lending, in G. D. Johnson, K. D. Thomas, A. K.

Harrison and S. A. Grier (eds), *Race in the Marketplace: Crossing Critical Boundaries*. Cham, Switzerland: Palgrave Macmillan, pp. 173–92.

Persky, J. (1995) The Ethology of Homo Economicus, *Journal of Economic Perspectives*, 9/2: 221–31.

Peterson, R. A., and Kern, R. M. (1996) Changing Highbrow Taste: From Snob to Omnivore, *American Sociological Review*, 61/5: 900–7.

Pietrykowski, B. (2009) *The Political Economy of Consumer Behavior*. New York: Routledge.

Piketty, T., and Saez, E. (2003) Income Inequality in the United States, 1913–1998, *Quarterly Journal of Economics*, 118/1: 1–39.

Pittman, C. (2017) Shopping While Black: Black Consumers' Management of Racial Stigma and Racial Profiling in Retail Settings, *Journal of Consumer Culture*, 20/1: 3–22.

President's Materials Policy Commission (1952) *Resources for Freedom*, Vol. 1: *Foundations for Growth and Security*. Washington, DC: US Government Printing Office.

Pridmore, J., and Lyon, D. (2011) Marketing as Surveillance: Assembling Consumers as Brands, in D. Zwick and J. Cayla (eds), *Inside Marketing: Practices, Ideologies, Devices*. Oxford: Oxford University Press, pp. 115–36.

Princen, T. (2005) *The Logic of Sufficiency*. Cambridge, MA: MIT Press.

Pruitt, S. W., and Friedman, M. (1986) Determining the Effectiveness of Consumer Boycotts: A Stock Price Analysis of Their Impact on Corporate Targets, *Journal of Consumer Policy*, 9: 375–87.

Raynolds, L., and Long, M. (2007) Fair/Alternative Trade: Historical and Empirical Dimensions, in L. Raynolds, D. Murray and J. Wilkinson (eds), *Fair Trade: The Challenges of Transforming Globalization*. New York: Routledge, pp. 15–32.

Roberts, M. (1975) Reforming Economic Growth, in M. Olson and H. H. Landsberg (eds), *The No-Growth Society*. London: Frank Cass, pp. 119–38.

Rockström, J., et al. (2009) Planetary Boundaries: Exploring the Safe Operating Space for Humanity, *Ecology and Society*, 14/2, art. 32.

Ruskin, J., and Wilmer, C. ([1860] 1986) *Unto This Last and Other Writings*. New York: Penguin.

Samson, A. (2014) An Introduction to Behavioral Economics, in A. Samson (ed.), *The Behavioral Economics Guide 2014*, www.behavioraleconomics.com/the-be-guide/the-behavioral-economics-guide-2014/.

Sassatelli, R. (2007) *Consumer Culture: History, Theory and Politics*. London: Sage.

Sassatelli, R. (2010) Economic Theories of Consumption, in *Social and Economic Development*, Vol. VIII. Paris: Eolss, pp. 194–206.

Schefold, B. (1985) On Changes in the Composition of Output, in *Political Economy: Studies in the Surplus Approach*, 1/2, pp. 105–42.

Schor, J. (1998) *The Overspent American: Why We Want What We Don't Need*. New York: Basic Books.

Schor, J. (2007) In Defense of Consumer Critique: Revisiting the Consumption Debates of the 20th Century, *Annals of the American Academy of Political and Social Science*, 611: 16–29.

Schumacher, E. (1973) *Small is Beautiful: A Study of Economics as if People Mattered*. London: Blond & Briggs.

Schumpeter, J., ([1943] 2010) *Capitalism, Socialism and Democracy*. New York: Routledge.

Schwartz, B. (2004) *The Paradox of Choice: Why More is Less*. New York: Ecco.

Scitovsky, T. (1992) *The Joyless Economy: The Psychology of Human Satisfaction*. New York: Oxford University Press.

Sethuraman, R., Tellis, G., and Briesch, R. (2011) How Well Does Advertising Work? Generalizations from a Meta-Analysis of Brand Advertising Elasticity, *Journal of Marketing Research*, 48: 457–71.

Shafrin, J. (2010) Operating on Commission: Analyzing How Physician Financial Incentives Affect Surgery Rates, *Health Economics*, 19/5: 562–80.

Shammas, C. (2012) Standard of Living, Consumption, and Political Economy over the Past 500 Years, in F. Trentmann (ed.), *The Oxford Handbook of the History of Consumption*. New York: Oxford University Press, pp. 211–28.

Shepherd, R. J. (2011) Consumer Culture in East Asia, in

D. Southerton (ed.), *Encyclopedia of Consumer Culture*. Thousand Oaks, CA: Sage, pp. 248–9.

Sherman, R. (2018) "A Very Expensive Ordinary Life": Consumption, Symbolic Boundaries, and Moral Legitimacy among New York Elites 1, *Socio-Economic Review*, 16/2: 411–33.

Shill, G. H. (2019) Americans Shouldn't Have to Drive, but the Law Insists on It, *The Atlantic*, 9 July.

Shove, E., and Warde, A. (2002) Inconspicuous Consumption: The Sociology of Consumption, Lifestyle, and the Environment, in R. E. Dunlap et al. (eds), *Sociological Theory and the Environment: Classical Foundations, Contemporary Insights*. Lanham, MD: Rowman & Littlefield.

Simon, H. (1982) *Models of Bounded Rationality*. Cambridge, MA: MIT Press.

Smith, A. ([1776] 1976) *An Inquiry into the Nature and Causes of the Wealth of Nations*. Chicago: University of Chicago Press.

Smith, A. (1981) *An Inquiry into the Nature and Causes of the Wealth of Nations*. Indianapolis: Liberty Fund.

Snyder, R. C. (2008) What is Third-Wave Feminism: A New Directions Essay, *Signs*, 34/1: 175–96.

Stearns, P. (2001) *Consumerism in World History: The Global Transformation of Desire*. New York: Routledge.

Steffen, W., et al. (2015) Planetary Boundaries: Guiding Human Development on a Changing Planet, *Science*, 347/6223.

Stigler, G. J. (1950) The Development of Utility Theory, *Journal of Political Economy*, 58/4: 307–27.

Stigler, G. J. (1961) The Economics of Information, *Journal of Political Economy*, 69/3: 213–25.

Stillerman, J. (2015) *The Sociology of Consumption: A Global Perspective*. Cambridge: Polity.

Stock, R. (2017) Is Cadbury's in-House "Cocoa Life" the Same as Fairtrade?, www.stuff.co.nz/business/89720276/is-cadburys-inhouse-cocoa-life-the-same-as-fairtrade.

Strauss, S. (1924) Things Are in the Saddle, *Atlantic Monthly*, November, pp. 577–88.

Sun, G., Chen, J., and Li, J. (2017) Need for Uniqueness as a Mediator of the Relationship between Face Consciousness and Status Consumption in China, *International Journal of Psychology*, 52/5: 349–53.

Taylor, D., and Strutton, D. (2016) Does Facebook Usage Lead to Conspicuous Consumption?, *Journal of Research in Interactive Marketing*, 10/3: 231–48.

Thaler, R. (2008) Mental Accounting and Consumer Choice, *Marketing Science*, 27/1: 15–25.

Thomas, D. (2016) Is Cadbury's Move the End for Fair Trade?, www.bbc.com/news/business-38137480.

Thomas, L. (2018) Walmart Teams up with Ellen DeGeneres for New Denim-Focused Clothing Line, www.cnbc.com/2018/08/14/walmart-teams-up-with-ellen-degeneres-for-new-clothing-line.html.

Thompson, E. P. (1967) Time, Work-Discipline, and Industrial Capitalism, *Past and Present*, no. 38: 56–97.

Thoreau, H. (1854) *Walden; or, Life in the Woods*. Boston: Ticknor & Fields.

Tomlin, K. M. (2019) Assessing the Efficacy of Consumer Boycotts of U.S. Target Firms: A Shareholder Wealth Analysis, *Southern Economic Journal*, 86/2: 503–29.

Trentmann, F. (2009) Crossing Divides: Consumption and Globalization in History, *Journal of Consumer Culture*, 9/2: 187–220.

Trentmann, F. (2012) Introduction, in F. Trentmann (ed.), *The Oxford Handbook of the History of Consumption*. Oxford: Oxford University Press, pp. 1–22.

Trentmann, F. (2016) *The Empire of Things: How We Became a World of Consumers, from the Fifteenth Century to the Twenty-First*. New York: Allen Lane.

Trucost (2013) *Natural Capital at Risk: The Top 100 Externalities of Business*. London: Trucost.

Tversky, A., and Kahneman, D. (1981) The Framing of Decisions and the Psychology of Choice, *Science*, 211: 453–8.

Twitchell, J. B. (1999) Two Cheers for Materialism, *Wilson Quarterly*, 23/2: 16–26.

Tymoigne, É., and Wray, L. (2013) *Modern Money Theory 101: A Reply to Critics*, Working Paper no. 778. Annandale-on-Hudson, NY: Levy Economics Institute.

United Nations Conference on Trade and Development

(2018) *Review of Maritime Transport 2018*. Geneva: United Nations.

Veblen, T. ([1899] 1994) *Theory of the Leisure Class*. New York: Penguin.

Wakefield, J. (2019) Chill at 'Chella, www.thesun.co.uk/ tvandshowbiz/8738762/what-is-coachella-festival-history/.

Walmart (2020) Company Facts, https://corporate.walmart. com/newsroom/company-facts.

Walras, L. (1954) *Elements of Pure Economics*. London: Routledge.

Warde, A. (2017) *Consumption: A Sociological Analysis*. London: Palgrave Macmillan.

Waring, M. (1999) *Counting for Nothing: What Men Value and What Women are Worth*. Toronto: University of Toronto Press.

Weber, M. (1961) *General Economic History*. New York: Collier Books.

Wherry, F., Seefeldt, K., and Alvarez, A. (2019) *Credit Where it's Due: Rethinking Financial Citizenship*. New York: Russell Sage Foundation.

Wiedenhoft-Murphy, W. (2016) *Consumer Culture and Society*. Los Angeles: Sage.

Willets, M. M., and Schor, J. (2012) Does Changing a Light Bulb Lead to Changing the World? Political Action and the Conscious Consumer, *Annals of the American Academy of Political and Social Science*, 644/1: 160–90.

Wilson, E. ([1985] 2003) *Adorned in Dreams: Fashion and Modernity*. New Brunswick, NJ: Rutgers University Press.

Wood, S. (2006) On Language: Choice, in *Bitchfest: Ten Years of Cultural Criticism from the Pages of Bitch Magazine*. New York: Farrar, Straus & Giroux, pp. 144–7.

World Bank (2020) *World Development Indicators*, databank. worldbank.org.

World Economic Forum and Bain & Co. (2018) *Future of Consumption in Fast-Growth Consumer Markets: India*. Geneva: World Economic Forum.

Worster, D. (2016) *Shrinking the Earth: The Rise and Decline of American Abundance*. New York: Oxford University Press.

Zeisler, A. (2006) Plastic Passion: Tori Spelling's Breasts and Other Results of Cosmetic Darwinism, in *Bitchfest:*

Ten Years of Cultural Criticism from the Pages of Bitch Magazine. New York: Farrar, Straus & Giroux, pp. 256–60.

Zevin, A. (2019) Every Penny a Vote, *London Review of Books*, 15 August, pp. 27–30.

Zuboff, S. (2019) Surveillance Capitalism and the Challenge of Collective Action, *New Labor Forum*, 28/1: 10–29.

Zukin, S. (2005) *Point of Purchase: How Shopping Changed American Culture*. New York: Routledge.

Zwick, D., and Cayla, J. (2011) Introduction, in D. Zwick and J. Cayla (eds), *Inside Marketing: Practices, Ideologies, Devices*. Oxford: Oxford University Press, pp. 3–22.

Index